DESIGNERS' APARTMENTS in JAPAN
Architect-Designed
High-Rise CONDOMINIUMS

DESIGNERS' APARTMENTS in JAPAN
Architect-Designed High-Rise CONDOMINIUMS

目次 / Contents

序文 / Foreword	004
THE TOKYO TOWERS / THE TOKYO TOWERS	009
芝浦アイランド ケープタワー / Shibaura Island Cape Tower	025
ルネッサなんばタワー / Renaissa Namba Tower	035
小杉タワー / THE KOSUGI TOWER	039
ザ・センター東京 / The Center Tokyo	049
ローレルタワー難波 / Laurel Tower Namba	057
クロスタワー大阪ベイ / X-Tower Osaka Bay	061
ザ・タワー大阪 / The Tower Osaka	067
パークシティ武蔵小杉 / Park City Musashikosugi	079
ミッドサザン・レジデンス御殿山 / Mid Southern Residence Gotenyama	089

ローレルタワーサンクタス梅田 Laurel Tower Sanctus Umeda	097	HUQUE building MINAMISEMBA HUQUE building MINAMISEMBA	173
広尾 quarto HIROO quarto	105	OAZO ASHIYA OAZO ASHIYA	177
マリナゲートタワー cotton harbor Marina Gate Tower	109	北野アパート Apartment Kitano	181
タワーレジデンストーキョー Tower Residence Tokyo	115	WK玉造 WK Tamatukuri	184
ラゾーナ川崎レジデンス LAZONA Kawasaki Residence	125	ディナ DINa	187
パークシティ豊洲 Urban Dock Park City TOYOSU	133	La Wasison北野 La Wasison Kitano	190
Brillia Grande みなとみらい OCEAN&PARK Brillia Grande Minatomirai OCEAN&PARK	143	FLEG池尻 FLEG Ikejiri	193
みなとみらいミッドスクエア・ザ・タワーレジデンス M.M.MID SQUARE The Tower Residence	151	サンタアガータ Sant' Agata	197
是空同心 Zeque Doshin	160	略歴 Biographies	200
キャナルファーストタワー Canal First Tower	163	あとがき Afterword	206
匠空MINATOMACHI Syoque Minatomachi	169		

DESIGNERS' APARTMENTS in JAPAN
Architect-Designed High-Rise CONDOMINIUMS

序文
Foreword

清水文夫（チーム相田武文）
Fumio Shimizu (Team Takefumi Aida)

第一次世界大戦後間もなく、住宅市場には公的部門により様々な規制や直接供給などの市場介入がなされた。農村から都市への人口大移動の時代であり、絶対的な住宅不足の状況下において、公的部門による住宅の直接供給や持ち家政策を中心とした住宅政策が採択された。都市近郊の農地は細分化かつ再分配されて宅地となり、土地利用、所有についてほとんど野放しの状態であり、それが法外な土地、住宅価格とともに、醜悪としかいいようのない都市景観を生み、住み手はそこから派生する豊かさの実感の欠如を長い間味わってきた。そんな中で1970年頃、都心の中に狭い土地を使った空間利用に挑戦した建築家たちがいた。特に安藤忠雄の「住吉の長屋」と東孝光が個人の努力で建てた「塔の家」は神話になった。この都市型住宅の出現やさらに住み手が経験してきた世界の都市や空間のクオリティーなどがあいまって、1990年に入ると21世紀の日本人の住様式がどうなるのかが問われ始める。「デザイナーズマンションNo2」の序文で東孝光氏

Soon after the World War I, the public sector intervened in the housing market through various regulations and public housing supply. It was the period of great migration from rural areas to cities, and under the absolute shortage of houses, the Japanese government adopted housing policies mainly based on direct housing supply and home-ownership drives. Agricultural land in the suburban area was segmented, redistributed and turned to building lots, and land utilization and ownership were almost uncontrolled, resulting in ugly urban landscapes as well as outrageous land and housing prices and disabling residents to feel a sense of affluence for a long time. Despite the situation, there were architects who addressed challenges of creative and efficient use of small lots at the heart of the cities around 1970. Especially, "Row House in Sumiyoshi" by Tadao Ando and "Tower House" built thanks to personal efforts by Takamitsu Azuma became myths. The emergence of urban housing and experience of quality housing and spaces in the world led to the question raised in the 1990's of how the Japanese style of living should be in the 21st century. In fact, in the introduction to Designers' Apartments in Japan: Super Choice, Mr. Takamitsu Azuma wrote, "... the 21st century living

は「21世紀の住様式は一つではなく多様な家族形態の試みと結びついている。…現在進行している『デザイナーズアパートメント』の変革は、その立体的な空間性や規模の小ささ、高性能の設備ばかりではなく住様式と家族形態の再編の実験的なあらわれと見るべきだ」と語っている。

集合住宅の進化は公団、造成住宅地、公団型分譲マンション、建築家の都市型住宅など、それぞれの時代の節目節目で、住宅の質の向上に影響を与えてきた。そして近年、タワー型大規模マンションが「官、公、民」一体となって地上げ手法と組み合わせて、大きな街区を形成しながらサステイナブルな街づくりをテーマに居住快適性を実現する例が見られるようになった。これは今まで市街地の小さなエリアで脈略もなく自分勝手にスクラップアンドビルドを繰り返してきた時代から、ドラスティックに次のステージに移行させるステップになるかもしれない。湾岸地域にもし潤沢にマンション用地が用意できたとしても交通利便性に劣る物件が多く、顧客を満足させられない。いくらマンションの価格と広さ、デザイン、設備がよくても交通利便性と居住快適性を同時に満たさなければ優良物件とはいえない。もし「官、公、民」で大きなブロックをインフラと共に開発出来れば、現在点在する高層マンションも含めて地域全体の居住快適性と生活利便性を同時に向上させることができるかもしれない。そこには人々が集い、遊び、生活文化が花開き創造的に生きる街が広がるかもしれない。ヨーロッパの都市のような…ローマが次々に石造りの都市を造り、人々が住み、中世が訪れ、ルネサンスの息をし、近世・近代の産業革命の洗礼を受け工業化社会が到来しても、人々はこの都市の秩序を尊重し、愛したような豊かな「構造」が構築できるかもしれない。レンガ壁に囲まれた、薄暗い路地を歩いていると、突然広々としたピアッツァに出る。そこにはカフェがあり、人々が集い、談笑する風景がある。人々は舞台に立ってしまったかのような

---

styles have been tied with diversity in family compositions…It appears that the changes brought about by Designers Apartments in progress should represent experiments not only in architectural approaches such as three-dimensional spatial designs and small-scale developments but also in reorganizations of living styles and family compositions."

The evolution of apartments have affected the improvements of housing at each turning point of the history, as illustrated by the foundation of Japan Housing Corporation (JHC), housing land development, apartment houses constructed by JHC and urban housing designed by architects. In recent years, we have seen emerging large-scale high-rise tower condominiums to form larger town blocks and to build sustainable neighborhoods after buying up of parcels of land for consolidation and resale through collaborations among "the municipalities, public organizations and private sector". This might mark a drastic new step from inconsistent scrap-and-build constructions in small-scale areas in the town to a new approach for development. Even if sufficient lots are provided for condominiums in bay areas, many of them are inferior in terms of transportation convenience and cannot satisfy customers. Even if pricing, areas, designs and facilities are favorable, we cannot call any condominiums excellent unless they meet the requirements of transportation convenience and amenities at the same time. If "the municipalities, public organizations and private sector" can cooperate to develop large blocks of land together with their infrastructure, they may be able to improve amenities and convenience of living in not only these blocks but also currently scattered high-rise apartments at the same time. There, people may gather, play and cause a town where life culture and creative lifestyles bloom to grow. Like cities in Europe. The Romans built stone cities one after another. People lived in there through the Medieval Age and the Renaissance. Even after the industrial revolution in early modern and modern times and the coming of the industrial society, people have still respected the order of these cities and loved them. We may be able to establish such rich "structures". The image is like this: when one walks through a gloomy alley with brick walls, one comes across a wide piazza; there is a cafeterraces here people gather and have conversations; they somehow feel excited as if they were on stage.

高揚感を覚える。そのような素敵な街の相（physiognomy）を持った都市が構成されるかもしれない。

さて日本全国のマンション供給は2000年の183.784戸以後、減少傾向にあり明らかにピークアウトしている。大都市および周辺市街地を有する地域以外では供給が純化している。これは交通利便性と居住の快適性のバランスのとれた地域に供給が集中し、マンション適地でない地域では大きく減少している。つまり首都圏郊外でのマンション供給は激減して戸建てエリアへと変貌し、都心にマンション供給が集中して結果として供給量全体を減少させている。

本来マンションは業務性の高い地域に効率よく住むための居住形態である。現代の都市に備わった様々な施設を日常的に使いこなし、豊かな歴史や水辺の潤いや緑あふれる景観とともに、都市の利便性や快適性を享受し、職住接近の生活拠点を持つことである。バブル期の地価高騰によって郊外にスプロールしたマンション需要が、バブル崩壊の地価下落を受けて東京都心部などの供給適地に回帰した。今後のマンションに対する需要は基本的には事業集積地とその周辺に集約される可能性が高く、交通利便性に劣る地域でのマンション供給はさらに減少すると思われる。つまり、マンション需要は、これまで以上に「交通利便性」と「居住快適性」という二つの条件によるところが大きくなってきた。では、居住快適性に求められている条件とは何か。立地する周辺環境の魅力、つまり地上の緑地や水辺をうまく取り込み、日常生活をサポートする生活利便施設であるカフェ、レストラン、医療施設があったり、さらに世代の垣根を越えて人と人がふれあえる街を擁すること。また土地の歴史性や文化性も加味して周辺住宅にも寄与していること、そして長期間居住に耐え得る様々な家族像に対応した

The new evolution presents possibilities of building cities combined with such an attractive physiognomy.

With 183,784 units in 2000 at its peak, the supply of apartments in Japan has continuously been reduced and has clearly peaked out. With the exceptions of the large cities and those areas having suburbs, the supply has constantly indicated a downward trend. In other words, the supply has concentrated upon the areas where transportation convenience and amenities of living are well-balanced and has drastically decreased in the areas not appropriate for apartment construction; the suburbs of the metropolitan area where the supply of apartments has greatly been reduced have turned into those of stand-alone houses while the apartment construction has concentrated upon the heart of Tokyo, consequently reducing the total supply.

Essentially, apartments are a form of housing that enables residents to efficiently live in or near business districts. Living in apartments means to take advantage of various advantage of facilities provided for modern cities in everyday life, to enjoy convenience and amenity of cities as well as rich histories, comfort at the waterfront and landscapes rich in green and to establish a base for life with close placement of residence and work place. Condominiums once moved out to the suburbs because of soaring land prices in the bubble economy have returned to areas suitable for land development at the heart of Tokyo and other locations after the collapse of the bubble. In the future, demand for condominiums is highly likely to concentrate upon business centers and surrounding areas while demand in areas with insufficient transportation convenience will further decrease. In other words, demand for condominiums depends on transportation convenience and amenities for living more than ever.

Then what are requirements for amenities? There are many: attractiveness of surrounding environments or presence of towns carefully taking advantage of green space and waterfront as part of landscapes, having cafe terraces, restaurants and medical facilities that support daily life and contribute to convenience of living and enabling people to contact and exchange with each

間取りや設備が備わっていること。各マンションデベロッパーは様々な企画、デザインを凝らし顧客のニーズをつなぎ止めてきた。サービスアパートメント（家具付き高級賃貸アパート）や顧客を特定する手法、例えば高齢者向けの介護、医療設備のある賃貸マンション。都市型コンパクトマンション、狭義でのデザイナーズマンション、分譲住宅と賃貸住宅を併設して世代の循環と世代間交流と促す方法などがあげられる。しかし（湾岸地域に）多くの物件が同様のスタイルで林立するだけでは、顧客のニーズをこれ以上つなぎ止めておくことは困難かもしれない。今日、誰もがデザインについて語り、誰もがファッション、ライフスタイル、生活文化を語るようになった。そして街並や景観についても関心が高まり、単なる建物のフォルムのデザインだけでは満足できなくなってしまった。統一感のある街並や景観、街全体のイメージこそ重要だと理解し始めた。顧客に対するニーズは今まで以上に多様化し、かつ高度化している。このような成熟したマーケットにあって、一部では顧客ニーズに合わない商品の売れ行きが鈍る例も見られている。多様化したマーケットの中で適切にそれぞれのニーズを捉えるマーケティング力やそれを具現化する商品企画力が一段と重要になってきている。しかし単なる市場リサーチだけで解決できるものではない。単に様々な顧客のニーズに応えるテイストの幅広さだけでもない。多くのデベロッパーは営業面での前倒し主義におちいり、従来のパターンを繰り返しがちだ。しかし中にはチーム力を駆使し、小さな気づきの集合体から価値を膨らませ一般的には不可能だと思われる計画を、理想的な構想、プランへと導くデベロッパーも存在している。デザインは革新である。デザインは社会において新しく創造的であるものすべて、エンターテイメントを創造するすべてのものを意味する。この本にみられる実例も数多くそのような視点から、日本の大都市集合住宅にふさわしいものとして選ばれた。日本の都住環境の未来への発展の可能性を求めて終わりなきデザインの革新に期待したい。

---

other beyond generations; contribution to surrounding residences by incorporating history and culture of localities in architectural and landscaping designs; and provision of floor plans and facilities corresponding to different types of families and endurable for long-term living. Individual condominium developers have thought out many plans and designs to meet needs of customers. Some examples of such approaches include service apartments (high-grade, furnished apartments for rent) and other condominiums for specific customers (for example, apartments for rent provided with nursing and medical services for the aged citizens); compact-sized, city apartments; designers apartments in a narrow sense; and method to provide apartments for sale and for rent in a structure to promote life cycles and exchanges among generations. It may be difficult however to satisfy customers' needs any more if many similar buildings are just built (in bay areas.) Today, everyone talks about design and discusses fashion, lifestyles and life culture. People have more and more interest in townscapes and landscapes and cannot be satisfied simply with the design of architectural forms. They have started to realize that what is important is consistent townscapes, landscapes and total images of the towns. Customers' needs are becoming more and more diversified and sophisticated. In such a mature market, we can even see some examples where sales of products not fitting customers' needs have dropped. Increasing importance are marketing capabilities to properly grasp individual needs in the diversified market and product planning to implement these needs. This cannot be solved through simple market researches. A wide range of offerings to meet different tastes won't do to meet the needs. Many developers tend to follow precedents in terms of sales and repeat the conventional patterns of actions. But there are some developers that take advantage of teamwork, create values from a collection of small facts they are aware of and turn ideas that are thought generally impossible into ideal concepts, plans and projects. Design is innovation. Design means everything new and creative and everything that generate entertainment in the society. The actual examples covered in the book are selected from the above-described viewpoint, as considered appropriate representatives of condominiums in large cities in Japan in the hope that ever-ongoing design innovations will contribute to development of urban living environments in the future.

企画
Executive Editor
大田 悟（グラフィック社）
Satoru Ota

エディトリアル・ディレクター
Editorial Director
清水 文夫
Fumio Shimizu

装丁デザイン
Cover Design
スズキeワークス
SUZUKI e WORKS

本文デザイン
Book Design
丹治 竜一
Ryuichi Tanji

協力
Cooperation
内田 浩史
Hiroshi Uchida

鈴木 隆子
Ryuko Suzuki

THE TOKYO TOWERS
THE TOKYO TOWERS

ORIX Real Estate Corporation / Tokyu Land Corporation / Sumitomo Corporation / Funakoshi Yasuhiro
Keita Ito / Hisakazu Fujita / Kaoru Tomosawa / Hiroyuki Nomura & Toru Horie / Koichi Ando
Masamichi Katayama / Gwenael Nicolas / Sumitomo Corporation

Data

Title
The Tokyo Towers

Developer
ORIX Real Estate Corporation
Tokyu Land Corporation
Sumitomo Corporation

Facade & Landscape
Funakoshi Yasuhiro
(Yamashita Sekkei Inc.)

Landscape
Keita Ito (Yamashita Sekkei Inc.)

Landscape & Lighting
Hisakazu Fujita (sola associates)

Public Space
Kaoru Tomosawa
(NIKEEN SPACE DESIGN Ltd.)

Public Lighting
Hiroyuki Nomura & Toru Horie
(Worktecht Corporation)

Lounge & Guest room Produce
Koichi Ando (ANDO GALLERY)

Lounge & Guest room Design
(Sea Tower) : Masamichi Katayama
(Wonderwall Inc.)
(Sky Tower) : Gwenael Nicolas
(CURIOSITY Inc.)

Architect
Sumitomo Corporation

Location
Chuo-ku, Tokyo

Site area
29,718.37m²

Building area
20,653.94m²

Total floor area
383,340.34m²

Structure
RC (S in part)

Completion
January, 2008

Materials
Exterior Wall :
45x90tile, sprayed coating
227x60 tile
Public Wall :
natural stone, polyvinyl chloride film
Public Floor :
natural stone

Photo
(Guest room) :
DAICI ANO

	2	3
1	4	5
	6	

1
ミッドロビー：2層吹抜けの開放的な空間で、大きなガラスウォールから光をたっぷり取り込む
Mid Lobby: This expansive 2-story well space fully takes in light.

2
「THE TOKYO TOWERS」の敷地エントランスである「ミッド・ゲート」
The "Mid Gate" serves as the entrance to the site of "THE TOKYO TOWERS".

3
セントラルパークの大階段。緑を配置し、広場のように演出されたスペース
The big stairway to the Central Park is arranged with green glass and luxurious trees.

4
エントランスへと導くアプローチ。弧を描く柱の連続が印象的なエアリーコリドー
The approach leading up to the entrance is designed as an airy with a series of impressive arching columns.

5
アクアステージ：水盤の水とガラスのキャノピーがライティングされ、空間に透明感を演出
Aqua Stage: Water in the pool and the glass canopies are highlighted by the light to give a sense of transparency in the space.

6
自然の色を映す照明が優しく迎えるミッドタワー・プライベートラウンジ
The private lounge of the Mid Tower welcomes everyone with naturally lit colors.

1	2	5
	3	6
	4	7

1
斬新かつ繊細な空間が広がるシータワー・プライベートラウンジ
The private lounge of the Sea Tower integrates novelty with delicacy in its space.

2
光と水の煌めきがひそむモダンテイストのシーロビー。緑がかった石貼りの壁が落ち着いた雰囲気を醸す
The Sea Lobby with a modern taste secretly accommodates sparkling light and resplendent water. Greenish stone-covered walls give a comfortable atmosphere.

3
シースカイラウンジ：日常でありながら非日常感覚の驚きが得られる遊び心に富んだラグジュアリー空間
Seasky Lounge: This luxurious space designed with imaginativeness always gives a surprise in the daily context.

4
シースカイラウンジ：ガラスウォールに面した部分は2層吹抜けとし、台場を一望する景色を存分に楽しめる
Seasky Lounge: The space by the glass walls is in the 2-story well to fully enjoy the grand view of Odaiba.

5
東京湾を望むスポーツ棟、シーサイドアネックス
The Seaside Annex, the building for sports, offers an excellent view of the Tokyo Bay.

6
25m屋内プール：ガラス張りの開放的な空間
25-meter indoor pool: Spacious, glass-enclosed space

7
ミッドスカイゲスト-2：上階には天然石貼りのバスルームを配置している。ガラスの色彩が湯面を揺らし、ファンタジックなバスタイムをリザーブする。枠組みにとらわれない独創的なデザイン
Midsky Guest-2: The upstairs has a bathroom using natural stone. The color of the glass is reflected upon the water to create a fantastic bathtime. This design is inspired, unconventional and original.

都心に新しい住宅エリアを創造する中央区のウォーターフロント・勝どき。住みやすさを追求した大規模な都市開発。都心という利便性と、水辺の潤いに恵まれた約29700㎡の敷地では、水と緑溢れる美しい景観を創造し、運河沿いには親水デッキを整備するなど、立地の潤いを十分に取り入れた環境づくりを行う。都心に位置しながらも雄大な海を望む環境は、高層建築が乱立する過密エリアとは異なり、伸びやかにそして充分な存在感で周囲にそのファサードを印象づけることができる。TOKYOのどこよりも高い空に姿を現す高層部には、超高層ゆえの建物のボリューム感を和らげる涼やかなカラーを採用している。空へ向かって穏やかに伸びる錆浅葱（さびあさぎ）色のカーブには、遠くからでも視認できるよう、フィンを連続的に設置。カーブをいっそう際立たせる。そのカーブの下、中層部にかけては、ホワイトのタイルで統一し、カーブの上はグレーからホワイトへのグラデーションで風の流れや帆の揺らぎを表現している。さらに陸から空へ、タワーの四隅を真っ直ぐ走るガラスのカーテンウォールや、バルコニーの手摺に用いたガラスとアルミの素材感。それらが、透明感のある現代的な表情を建物に添えてくれる。東京で最も空高く、大きな帆を掲げて未来へと進む2つのタワー。その姿は、この都市が大きな潤いを懐に抱きながら発展を遂げてゆく姿を、遠くから眺める人々の目にもしっかりと印象づけていくだろう。

Kachidoki is at the waterfront of Chuou-ku in the process of redevelopment of a new residential area adjacent to downtown Tokyo. In this area, urban designing is widely promoted in pursuit of life's convenience. Having convenience of capital city and elegant richness of waterside, the site of approximately 29,700m2 offers beautiful landscape abundant in water and green. A pleasant environment is developed with careful concerns for the creation of the landscape fully adopted the water grace of the situation as exemplified by the seaside deck along a canal. Although located in the center of the capital city, the Tokyo Towers commanding a magnificent view of the sea is definitely different from the surrounding areas with high-rise building standing close together and is capable of impressing the facade favorably upon the surroundings with its unrestricted and dignified presence. The upper floors in the highest sky of Tokyo adopt the light colors that soften the oppressiveness inherent to the volumes of high-rise buildings. Towards the sky extend curves in the color of light teal blue, and the curves are continuously finned for recognition and further emphasis when seen from the distance. Down from the curve to the middle levels, the exterior walls are all tiled in white while above the curves is the gradation of tiles from gray to white expressing the passing wind and billowing sails. Moreover, giving prominence to their material presences are glass curtain walls installed straight along the tower's four corners from the ground to the sky as well as the glass and aluminum used for the railings of balconies. These elements add transparent modern impression to the towers. Highest up in the Tokyo sky, the two towers hoist sails and enjoy a cruise into the future. Their figures will appear as symbols of this still growing city with elegance in the eyes of people even from a distance.

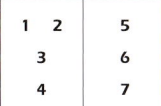

1
ミッドスカイラウンジ：エントランスの左右は緑のガラスをはめこみ、神秘的な雰囲気で別世界へ誘う
Mid Sky Lounge: Green glass panels are arranged to the left and right of the entrance, giving a mystic atmosphere and inviting to another world.

2
ミッドスカイラウンジ：天然石貼りの床に円形カーペットを敷き、モダンなソファーを配置
Mid Sky Lounge: A round carpet is laid on the floor tiled with natural stone, and sofas with a modern design are arranged on it.

3
ミッドスカイゲスト-2：透明感のあるピンクのガラスで部分的に仕切り、魅惑的な視界を創る
Mid Sky Guest-2: The space is partially partitioned with semitransparent pink glass panels for creating an attractive view.

4
ミッドスカイゲスト-1：クリアガラスで仕切られたベールの中にバーカウンターをレイアウト
Mid Sky Guest-1: A bar counter is installed in the space partitioned with clear glass panels.

5
シースカイゲスト：部屋の一面をガラスのカーテンウォールとしたメゾネットタイプになっている
Seasky Guest: A glass curtain wall is used for one side of the room designed as a maisonnette.

6
シースカイゲスト：吹抜けの開放的な空間でくつろげるジャグジー・スペース
Seasky Guest: This space with a Jacuzzi in a well is best suitable for relaxation.

7
シースカイゲスト：リビング＆ベッドコーナー：間接照明が心地よい安らぎを与える
Seasky Guest: In this living and bed area, indirect lighting contributes to a sense of comfort.

Sensibility
Sensibility

Masako Hamada (Hamada Design Works) / Takeharu Saki (Office SAKI)

Data

Title
Sensibility

Producer
Masako Hamada
(Hamada Design Works)

Designer
Takeharu Saki (Office SAKI)

Area
165.43m²

Materials
Interior Wall :
 natural stone, tile, cloth
Interior Floor :
 natural stone, flooring, carpet

Photo
Takeshi Nakasa

1
創造を遥かに超えた広さを備えたリビングルーム
The living room is much wider than one might expect.

2
ホワイエからダイニングスペースを臨む
The dining space seen from the foyer

3
ダイニングスペース、ホワイエを臨む。奥にキッチンを配している
The dining space and foyer. The kitchen is arranged at the back.

4
エレガントな時間を演出する優雅なリビング・ダイニングルーム
This graceful living/dining room takes one to a time of elegance.

5
キッチンからダイニングスペースを臨む
The dining space seen from the kitchen

玄関ホールの水のスクリーンが至福の時のはじまりを告げる。インテリアの落ち着いたカラーとガラスやミラーの透明感が、均整を保って調和するリビング・ダイニング。深い奥行きと窓の外に広がる眺望に吸い込まれるように、心は解放を手に入れていく。夕暮れとともに、一層美しさを増すTOKYOの街を眼下に見ながら、まるで夜間飛行を楽しむような天上の住処。手に入れた世界の美しさに酔いしれる夜を、この場所がドラマチックに演出する。

The water screen at the entrance hall marks the beginning of prime time. In the living and dining area, quiet colors of the interior and transparency of glasses and mirrors presents a well-balanced harmony. As if to be drawn into the depth of the room and a view spreading outside the window, one feels a sense of freedom. With twilight, the city of Tokyo adds more charms to its beauty, and seeing the city below from this heavenly place, one can feel as if one were taking a night flight. Carried away by the beauty at hand in a pall of darkness in the night dramatically produced by this place.

```
1
2 3
4
```

1
凛とした心地よい緊張感のあるエントランスホール
The awe-inspiring entrance hall gives a comfortable sense of tension.

2
パウダールーム：2ボウルタイプのワイドな洗面化粧台には重厚な天然石仕様のカウンタートップを採用し、格調高い雰囲気を醸している
Powder room: The wide dresser with two sinks employs massive natural stone counter top, giving a refined atmosphere.

3
ベッドルーム：間接照明やテクスチャーのある素材を使った、ゆとりと品位に満たされた空間
Bedroom: The roomy, elegant space uses indirect lighting and textured materials.

4
バスルーム
Bathroom

Kehai
Kehai

Masako Hamada(Hamada Design Works) / Kayoko Shimada (Island alpha)

1

1
リビング・ダイニング：床の間に見立てた壁が和の美意識を感じさせる
Living/dining space: The wall compared to an alcove inspires a delicate sense of beauty.

Data

Title
 Kehai

Producer
 Masako Hamada
  (Hamada Design Works)

Designer
 Kayoko Shimada (Island alpha)

Area
 113.47m²

Materials
 Interior Wall :
  natural stone, plastered wall, cloth
 Interior Floor :
  natural stone, flooring

Photo
 Noboru Morikawa

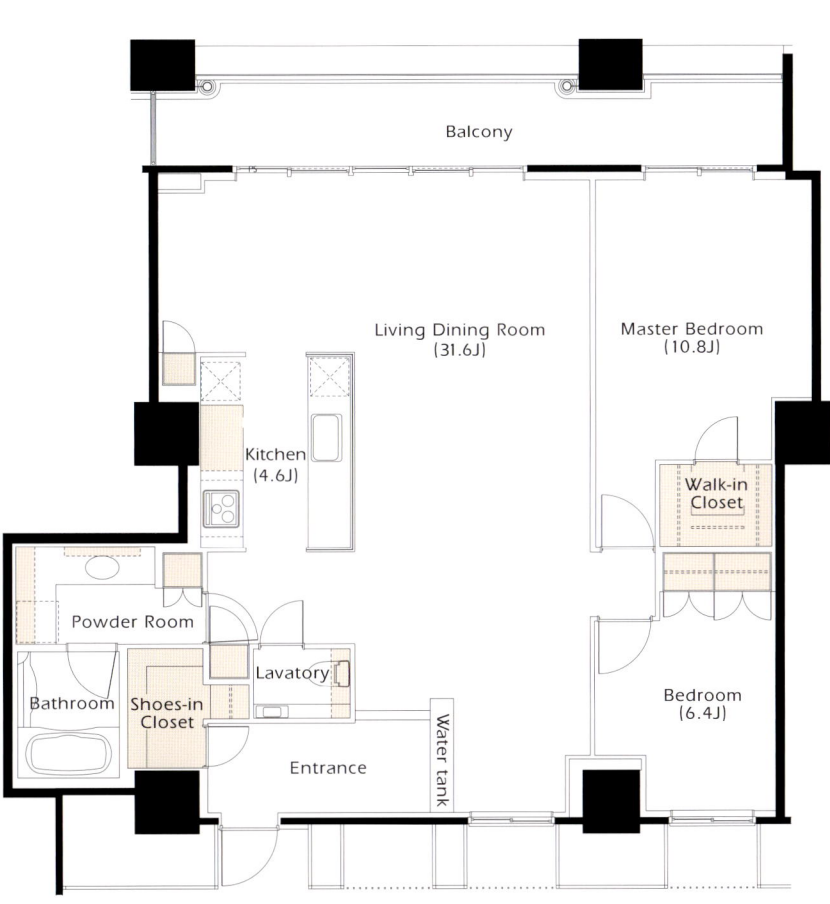

1	4
2	5
3	6

1
おもてなしの赤を用いたエントランス
The entrance in red expresses a welcoming spirit.

2
リビングスペース：スタッコ調の塗り壁や間接照明が風情のある安らぎを与える
In this living space, stucco-finish painted walls and indirect lighting results in a refined elegance.

3
キッチンからダイニングを臨む。キッチンのガラスウォールはクリアとスモークを切り替えられる
The dining room seen from the kitchen whose glass walls can be switched between clear ones and smoked ones.

4
和の趣で落ち着いた雰囲気のマスターベッドルーム
The Japanese taste of the master bedroom creates a sense of comfort and relaxation.

5
ダイニングスペース
Dining space

6
ベッドルーム
Bedroom

互いの気配が、家族を心地よい距離感で結んでいく。リビング・ダイニング、キッチン、書斎スペースを仕切りのない一室とするプランニング。時にはプライベート性を高められるよう、キッチンの間仕切りは、クリアとスモークを切り替えられるガラスウォールにするなど、個々の時間を尊重する配慮も。気配という奥ゆかしい美意識がモダンなコーディネートに馴染むのは、ファニチャーを床の間に見立てたレイアウトや、玄関にもてなしの赤色を用いた色づかいなど、所々に日本の心が息づいているからかもしれない。

Feeling each other's presence in a comfortable distance, the family can enjoy life in this unit type. The living-dining area, kitchen and study are all integrated into a single space without partition. To flexibly adjust the extent of privacy, the partition with the kitchen, for example, employs a glass wall that can be switched between clear glass and frosted one, paying respect to each and every moment. The modest aesthetic sense of sign (Kehai) still matches this modern coordination because of the Japanese spirit carefully applied to details including the layout comparing the furniture to Japanese alcove (Tokonoma) and the coloring of the entrance using the red to represent a welcoming atmosphere.

Transit
Transit

Masako Hamada(Hamada Design Works) / Katsuyuki Sakoh (OKANOUE)

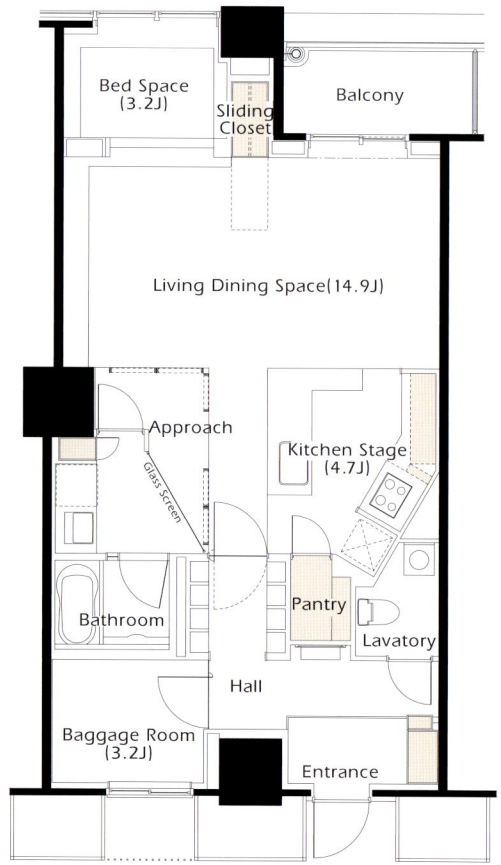

Data
Title
  Transit
Producer
  Masako Hamada
  (Hamada Design Works)
Designer
  Katsuyuki Sakoh (OKANOUE)
Area
  70.78m²
Materials
  Interior Wall :
   tile, cloth
  Interior Floor :
   flooring, tile
Photo
  DAICI ANO

	2	4
1	3	
	5	

1
ダイナミックなパターンの壁が印象的なリビングスペース
The walls with dynamic patterns give a strong impression in this living space.

2
ガラススクリーンで仕切られたバスルーム
The bathroom is partitioned with a glass screen.

3
ダイニングスペースからキッチン、アプローチを臨む
The kitchen and approach seen from the dining space

4
アプローチからリビングスペースを臨む。奥にはベッドルームを配している
The living space seen from the approach. The bedroom is set up at the back.

5
キッチンステージ
Kitchen stage

|1|
|2|
|3 4|

1
リビングスペースからベッドスペースを臨む
The bedroom seen from the living space

2
バッゲージルーム
Baggage room

3
エントランスホール
Entrance hall

4
黒を基調としたシックなラボラトリー
Chic black-based lavatory

この街で生きるテンションとモチベーションを、プライベートな時間でさえ保ち続けていたい。そんなTOKYOを求める気持ちに、この空間が応える。フルスケルトンの斬新なレイアウトで、魅せる、キッチン、リビング、バスルーム。ウォールを埋め尽くすダイナミックなパターン。ガラスやミラー、ひとつひとつのオブジェが繰り広げるトリックに満ちた空間。全ては、くつろぎの中にもインスピレーションを求める住まい手の、クリエイティブな生き方を強く主張する。ここは、目指すものがある人の、寄港地のようなTOKYO。

If you want to maintain pace and motivation in your life in Tokyo even during private time, this is the room you've been looking for. The kitchen, living space and bathroom are all radically implemented with translucent materials and structures. Dynamic patterns cover the walls. Each space is full of tricks of glasses, mirrors and other objects. Everything appeals to a creative life of each resident who seeks for inspirations even in the time of comfort. This is the shape of Tokyo to come as a port of call for ones with aims.

芝浦アイランド ケープタワー
Shibaura Island Cape Tower

Mitsui Fudosan Co., Ltd. / Mitsubishi Corporation / ORIX Real Estate Corporation / Sumitomo Corporation
Nippon Steel City Produce, Inc. / ITOCHU Property Development, Ltd. / Jun Mitsui / KAJIMA Corporation

Data

Title
Shibaura Island Cape Tower

Developer
Mitsui Fudosan Co., Ltd.
Mitsubishi Corporation
ORIX Real Estate Corporation
Sumitomo Corporation
Nippon Steel City Produce, Inc.
ITOCHU Property Development, Ltd.

Design Coordinator
Jun Mitsui

Architect
KAJIMA Corporation

Location
Minato-ku, Tokyo

Site area
16,908.83m²

Building area
7,842.19m²

Total floor area
140,004.31m²

Structure
RC

Completion
December, 2006

Materials
Exterior Wall :
  45x90 ceramic tile, 227x60 tile, paint
Public Wall :
  marble, limestone, paint
Public Floor :
  granite, flooring

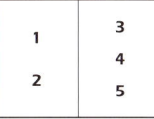

1
ホテルライクな車寄せも備えたワイドなガラス面がモダンなメインエントランス
The modern-looking Main Entrance with wide glass walls also features a porch like that of a high-grade hotel.

2
敷地配置図
Site Plan

3
プライベートガーデン：ウォーターガーデンを中心に緑が半円状に広がっている居住者専用のアウトドアスペース
Private garden: This outdoor space exclusive for residents has a fan-shaped expansion of a garden around the Water Garden.

4
水面の向こうに緑が広がっている。そんな景色が楽しめるウォーターガーデン
In the Water Garden, one can see trees beyond the pond.

5
ベンチのあるノードや近道ができるフットパス
A node with a bench and a footpath for shortcut

1
フォーマルなメインエントランスに対し、カジュアルなガーデンエントランス。割石調の床や割肌調の柱など、自然色の強い表情のある素材を採用し、プライベートガーデンとの一体感を強調
This casual Garden Entrance forms a striking contrast with the formal Main Entrance. The floor with a touch of rag-stone and the columns having a chopped face impression represents the key selections of natural taste materials highlighting the integrity with the private garden.

2
ベンチやBGM、また希少なアラバスター（雪花石膏：光を通す石）を使った花器で演出されたエレベーターホール
The elevator hall is arranged with a set of benches, background music and a vase made of precious alabaster (translucent in light).

3
ウェルカムカスケード（滝）：エントランスホール中央に備えた滝。水音がやさしく人を迎えます
Welcome Cascade: This small waterfall is located at the center of the Entrance Hall, welcoming people with soft sounds of running water.

Shibaura Island Cape Tower | 027

穏やかな海、大きな空、そして人の暮らし。「芝浦アイランド」は、海と空と、そこに住まう人の暮らしをつなぐ、都心の島。そしてこの島を象徴する島内最大規模タワーレジデンスが、「芝浦アイランド」の「岬（cape）」ともいえる、島の最南端に位置する「ケープタワー」。建物の3方を運河に囲まれているため、建物のまわりに十分なスペースがあり、圧倒的な開放感がある。最南端であることから、日照条件も良好。対岸の建物が比較的低いため、都心でもプライバシーを保て、さまざまな方位に視界の良い眺望が広がる。「芝浦アイランド」は大小多彩な性格のオープンスペースと、島全周の遊歩道のネットワークによって外部空間を形成。その中でも圧倒的な面積をしめる広場・歩行空間の路面には、できるだけ自然素材のレンガや石を使用し、島全体に温もりある雰囲気を演出。すべての超高層タワーは、低層、中層、上層部の3層構成の外観デザインを共用。低層部には重厚感のあるブラウン系の色調を採用。中層部は、オレンジや黄色などの明るいアースカラー。高層部には、ホワイトやシルバーのマテリアルをデザイン。大地と調和する建物が、上層に向かって軽快な表情に変わり、空に続いていくというイメージで構成されている。

A calm sea, a splendid blue sky, and a life in the Metropolitan Tokyo; the "Shibaura Island" is a residential block built on an isle centrally located in the city of Tokyo, establishing connections between the residents' lives and the sea and the sky. And the landmark of the isle is its largest tower residence, Shibaura Cape Tower, located at the southern end or the "Cape" of the Shibaura Island. Since three sides of the building face a canal, there is sufficient open space around the building, giving an overwhelming sense of spaciousness. As the building is at the south end of the isle, the tower enjoys a very favorable sunshine condition. Across the river stand relatively low buildings, which results in a high level of privacy of the residents despite its location at the heart of the city while magnificent views extend in all directions. The outside space of the "Shibaura Island" comprises of open spaces of various sizes and different characteristics and a network of promenades around the perimeter of the Island. Especially, plazas and sideways that take up most of the outside space are paved with bricks and stones of natural materials wherever possible to produce a warm atmosphere. All the high-rise buildings on the isle share the similar exterior design dividing the building into the lower, middle and upper parts. The podium of the building has a dignified shade of brown; the middle part adopts rich, saturated earth colors such as orange and yellow; the top floors employ white or silver materials. The concept of the tower is that a building in perfect harmony with the ground gradually changes its appearance to a light one towards the top as if it were melting into the sky.

P150-A type, P90-A type
P150-A type, P90-A type
Yukio Hashimoto

1

豊かな眺望と、たっぷりの採光が降り注ぐリビング・ダイニング。ガラス越しにバスルームを臨む

Bathed in the bright sunshine, the living-dining room offers a magnificent command of view. The bathroom can be seen beyond the glass.

ケープタワーのインテリアプランには、自然に近いやわらかさや変化を持った空間構成に、自然をイメージしたカラーやマテリアルを多用している。ここには、身も心もゆるやかに暮らせる「裸の生活」がある。そんな自然な状態を楽しめる生活にこそ、これからの日本人のステイタスがあるのではないかと考えている。

(橋本夕紀夫)

In designing the interior of the Cape Tower, the spatial structure with flexibility and variations as seen in nature is combined with many nature-inspiring colors and materials. The building offers a "naked life" that ensures a relaxed life for both body and soul, and I think that such natural way of living suggests the way the Japanese in the future should be.

(Yukio HASHIMOTO)

Data

Title
P150-A type

Designer
Yukio Hashimoto

Area
150.58m²

Materials
Interior Wall :
  marble, vinyl cloth
Interior Floor :
  marble, flooring, carpet, bamboo granite

Title
P90-A type

Designer
Yukio Hashimoto

Area
88.33m²

Materials
Interior Wall :
  vinyl cloth
Interior Floor :
  marble, flooring

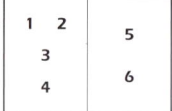

1
P-150-A-type：自然素材を採り入れ、高級感とやさしさを兼ね備えたエントランスホール
P-150-A-type : The entrance hall employs natural materials, giving a sense of quality and gentleness.

2
P-150-A-type：ダイニングルーム
P-150-A-type : Dining room

3
P-150-A-type：ホームシアターが楽しめる、やさしい雰囲気のプライベートルーム
P-150-A-type : This relaxing private room is equipped with a home theater system.

4
P-150-A-type：プライベートルーム：間接照明で演出されたスタディルーム
P-150-A-type : Private room: Indirect lighting gives a quality atmosphere to this study.

5
P-150-A-type：マスターベッドルーム：竹の床材や、縦格子のパーティションで仕切られるコンサバトリーなど、京都の落ち着いたホテルのような雰囲気を醸し出す
P-150-A-type : Master bedroom: Floored with bamboo and having a conservatory partitioned with lattice walls, this room has an impression of a hotel in Kyoto.

6
P-150-A-type：天然石をふんだんに使用したパウダールーム
P-150-A-type : The powder room amply uses natural stone.

P150-A-type Plan

Shibaura Island Cape Tower

Shibaura Island Cape Tower

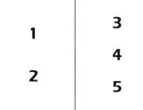

1
P-90-A-type：リビングからダイニング・キッチンを臨む。優雅なひとときを過ごせる、ゆとりと品位に満たされた空間
P-90-A-type : The dining room-cum-kitchen seen from the living room. It is a quality space with a sense of comfort, enabling residents to spend a time of elegance.

2
P-90-A-type：天然大理石を採用したエントランスホール
P-90-A-type : The entrance hall is floored with natural marble.

3
P-90-A-type：東京を一望できる風景やウッドデッキのバルコニーが、住空間に更なる開放感を演出している
P-90-A-type : A sense of openness in the living space is contributed to by a grand view of Tokyo and the wood deck balcony

4
P-90-A-type：ダイニング・キッチン：ダイニングテーブルの横にデザートやシャンパンなどを冷やせるパーティ・シンクが付随している
P-90-A-type : Dining room-cum kitchen: A party sink is provided near the dining table to cool deserts and a bottle of Champaign.

5
P-90-A-type：壁４面にライムストーン調のタイルを貼ったバスルーム。ひとクラス上の上質感に癒される空間
P-90-A-type : Four walls are covered with limestone-like tiles in the bathroom that lets residents feel a sense of quality time.

P90-A-type Plan

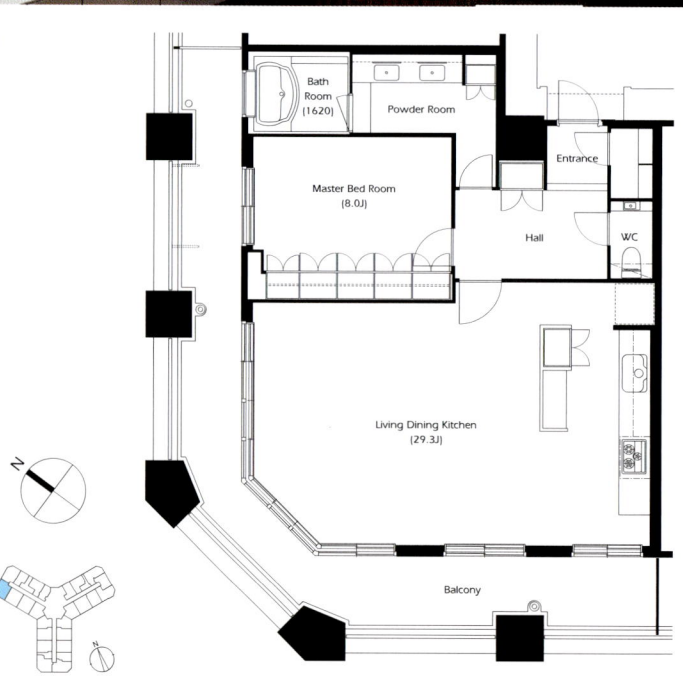

1

P-90-A-type：シックな雰囲気のマスターベッドルーム。半透明ガラスを採用したワイドクロゼットを配したゆとりある広さ

P-90-A-type : Master bedroom with a chic atmosphere. Having a wide-span closet with semitransparent glass doors, it gives a sense of spaciousness.

2

P-90-A-type：スライド式の大型ミラーを採用した、落ち着いた雰囲気のパウダールーム

P-90-A-type : This comfortable powder room employs a sliding large mirror.

ルネッサなんばタワー
Renaissa Namba Tower

MARUBENI Corporation / Tokyo Tatemono Co., Ltd. / Mitsubishi Estate Co., Ltd.
Keihan Electric Railway Estate Co., Ltd. / KAJIMA DESIGN KANSAI

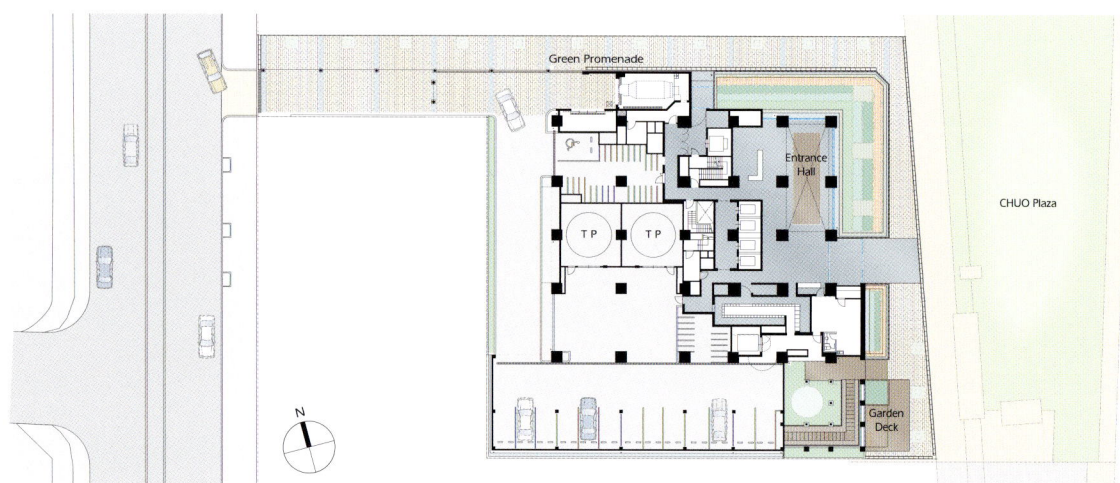

Data

Title
Renaissa Namba Tower

Developer
MARUBENI Corporation
Tokyo Tatemono Co., Ltd.
Mitsubishi Estate Co., Ltd.
Keihan Electric Railway Estate Co., Ltd.

Architect
KAJIMA DESIGN KANSAI
(Naoko Ohira)

Location
Naniwa-ku, Osaka city

Site area
3,000m²

Building area
1,670.69m²

Total floor area
38,104.06m²

Area
45.05-153.10m²

Structure
RC (S in part)

Completion
February, 2006

Materials
Exterior Wall :
  227x60tile, granite, sprayed coating
Public Wall :
  marble, sliced veneer
Public Floor :
  slate, granite, wood, flooring

Materials
Interior Wall :
  vinyl cloth
Interior Floor :
  flooring

Photo
Yoshiharu Matsumura

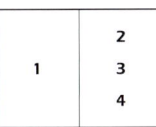

1
中央広場側に設けられたエントランス
The entrance is on the side of the central plaza.

2
中央広場との一体感を感じさせる開放的なエントランスホール。間接照明となっているガラス手摺が柔らかで落ち着いた雰囲気を演出
The entrance hall gives a sense of spaciousness and integrity with the central plaza. Indirectly lit glass railings give a soft and gentle impression.

3
エントランスホール：黒系を基調としたコンテンポラリーな空間を演出
Entrance hall: A black-based contemporary space

4
オーナーズサロン（2階）：吹抜け空間に面したくつろぎのスペース
wners' salon (2nd floor): A relaxing space faces the well.

JR難波駅を中心とした再開発地域「ルネッサなんば」に位置する38階建て、288邸の都市型超高層住宅である。再開発地域の核である「中央広場」を大きなプライベートガーデンと捉え、住まう人のメイン機能（エントランスホール、オーナーズサロン等）を中央広場沿いに配置している。新しく誕生した街との一体感や賑わいづくりに取り組むことで都市型住宅の提案を行なった建物である。外観は、装飾的要素を最小限に切り詰め「ミニマル」に徹し、住宅建築の雑然さを排除することに取り組んだ。単調になりがちな全周囲バルコニーを「パンチング・黒系ガラス・視線を制御する白系ガラス」と、竪格子で絡み合せた「面」構成とすることで、シンプルでかつ象徴性のあるフォルムを目指した。全体イメージをモノトーンで統一し、都市の進化を思わせるモダンなシルエットが都心のスカイラインに映えている。基壇部は、薄さを強調したアルミハニカムの庇と透明感を出したガラスの箱をイメージした下屋（風除室等）で構成されている。中央広場と連続した並木・間接照明の仕掛けを施したフレームに囲まれた植込みとの兼ね合いで、建物全体の高さからくる圧倒的な威圧感とは対象的に、人を拒まない優しい雰囲気を醸し出している。

This is a 38-story urban high-rise condominium having 288 units located in the "Renaissa Namba" redevelopment area around the JR Namba station. Based on the concept to regard the core of the area, "Central Plaza", as a private garden, the key residential functions (entrance hall, owners' salon, etc.) are arranged along the plaza. This proposal of an urban condominium emphasizes the integrity with a newly built town and its liveliness. "Minimal" decorations on the exterior are provided in order to eliminate untidiness typical to residential buildings. Balconies around the building that tend to appear dull are designed as planes by combining punched panels, black-based glass and white glass to limit direct line of sight views with vertical grilles, intended to have a simple and symbolic form. The overall impression is in monotone, and the modern silhouette suggesting the evolution of the city is reflected against the skyline at the heart of the city. The podium-level of the building is constituted by the aluminum honeycomb canopy emphasizing its thinness and windbreak and other public spaces inspiring transparent glass boxes. Thanks to the combination with the roadside trees that continue from the central plaza and plantations surrounded by the indirectly lit frames, the level gives a welcoming and familiar atmosphere in contrast with a sense of overwhelming presence of the building due to its height.

| 1 |
| 2 |
| 3 |

1-3
24階に設けられたスカイラウンジ：バーカウンター席から重厚なソファーまで備えた空間は夜の落ち着いた雰囲気を演出
Sky lounges on the 6th, 7th and 24th floors : These spaces equipped with furniture from counter seats to massive sofas offer a laid-back atmosphere at night.

小杉タワー
The Kosugi Tower

ITOCHU Property Development, Ltd. / Tokyo Tatemono Co., Ltd. / Joint Corporation Co., Ltd.
Jun Mitsui & Associates Inc. Architects / Freecs Co., Ltd. / TAISEI Corporation

地上49階建のタワーのデザインは、英国のハンプトンコートのような、繊細な素材感と、庭園と建物の調和を目指し、ひと目見るだけで従来の集合住宅とは一線を画す、斬新なデザインといえる。外壁のマテリアルには、レンガを意識した暖かみのあるタイルや、新しく変わる街の未来を感じさせるシルバーの素材、さらに多摩川の水や大きな空をイメージしたガラスといった多彩な素材を使用。近景や遠景、そして四方どの角度から眺めても美しさを感じられる、16種類のタイルによるリズミカルな色彩のグラデーションが綿密に施されている。再開発の最南端、ランドマークと呼ばれるに相応しい、存在感のあるファサードを構築している。空に向かって居住空間が広がるのに対して、その足下の大地には、ゆったり自然が広がる。ランドスケープデザインのコンセプトは、英国の風景式庭園がモチーフ。7つの異なるテーマのエリアに季節や色彩の異なる花や樹木を配し、そこを歩くだけで四季の心地よいリズムを感じられる日常を創造している。

The design of this 49-story tower is intended to offer a delicate sense of materials and a harmony between the garden and the architecture as found in Hampton Court in England, and its originality and difference from the conventional condominiums can easily be recognized at a glance. Diverse exterior wall materials include brick-like tiles giving a sense of warmth, silver-colored materials suggesting the future of the changing town and glass suggesting the water of the Tama river and big sky. In a short- or long-distance view or in a view from any angle, one can enjoy the building's architectural beauty. Color graduation with 16 types of tiles is applied with careful attention, giving an impression of rhythm. Located in the southern end of the redevelopment area, the tower reveals a facade appropriate for its presence as the landmark. While the residential units are built up toward the sky, a garden full of nature covers the ground. The concept of the landscape design is based on landscape style gardens in Britain. Flowers and trees with different flowering seasons or colors are planted in the seven areas with unique themes, and one can comfortably enjoy different colors by just taking a walk in it.

Data

Title
THE KOSUGI TOWER

Developer
ITOCHU Property Development, Ltd.
Tokyo Tatemono Co., Ltd.
Joint Corporation Co., Ltd.

Total Design Supervision
Jun Mitsui & Associates Inc. Architects

Plan Supervision
Freecs Co., Ltd.

Planting Design
Tetsuo Hanawa

Lighting Design
Satoshi Uchihara

Architect
TAISEI Corporation

Location
Kawasaki city, Kanagawa

Site area
11,856.76m²

Building area
2,849.84m²

Total floor area
81,680.30m²

Structure
RC

Completion
June, 2008

Materials
Exterior Wall :
  tile, sprayed coating
Public Wall :
  natural stone
Public Floor :
  natural stone, tile, flooring, carpet

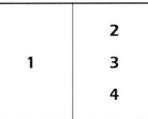

1
アプローチの両サイドに水盤を配したフォーマルエントランス。オニキスから光が漏れる重厚なキャノピーを設置したおもてなしの空間
The formal entrance has pools on both sides of the approach. A space welcomes residents and guests with a massive canopy where lights leak in through the onyx.

2
ローズガーデン：趣のあるレンガの舗装、バラのガゼボをイメージした美しい庭園が、ゲストを優雅に迎える
Rose garden: Beyond a sophisticated bricked path is a beautiful garden inspiring a rose gazebo gracefully welcomes guests.

3
ウォーターテラス：忙しい日常にひとときの安らぎをもたらす、さわやかな水面が広がるテラス
Water terrace: A terrace with a refreshing view of water surface gives a moment of comfort in a busy daily life.

4
夏の強い陽射しを和らげてくれる緑の木陰。気持ちのいい風が木立の間から吹き抜けるファミリーフィールド
Shades of green offer an escape from strong summer sunshine. A gentle breeze blows through the trees in the playground for families.

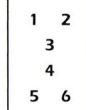

1

グランドテラスの中央には、床を柔らかく光らせ、水辺に浮かぶ船をイメージしてデザインしたステップ（階段の踊り場）を設置

Steps and a landing inspired by a ship on water are established at the center of the grand terrace, softly illuminating the floor.

2

フォーマルエントランスの扉の奥に広がる、二層吹き抜けの豪奢なグランドロビー。フロアは格調高いライムストーン貼り

The luxurious grand lobby is located in the two-story well behind the walls of the formal entrance. Flooring is covered with magnificent limestone.

3

グランドテラス：マナーハウスという共用スペースのコンセプトを象徴する美しく壮大なスペース

Grand terrace: Beautiful and expansive space symbolizes the "manor house" concept of the common spaces.

4

スカイラウンジ：一流ホテルのように格調高く洗練された、天空からの眺めを楽しめる特等席

Sky lounge: This magnificent and sophisticated space is equipped like a high-grade hotel, enabling one to enjoy a special view from the top of the building.

5

屋上庭園：タワー屋上に設置した、天空のガーデンスペース。街を優雅に見下ろし、遠くに霞む地平線まで見渡せる

Roof garden: Garden space in the sky is built on the roof of the tower. One can look down across the townscape and the hazy horizon beyond.

6

スカイスイート：ゲストの宿泊施設として、リラクゼーションバスを設置したゲストルーム

Sky Sweet: Guestroom is provided with a relaxation bath to accommodate guests.

The Kosugi Tower

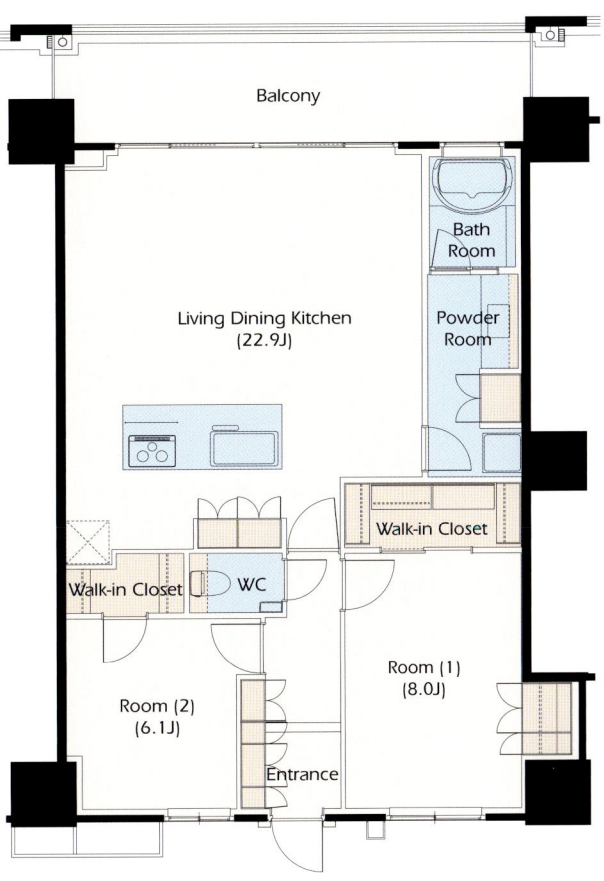

プレシャススタイル
Precious Style S90B-S type
Mami Mori

1

1
リビング・ダイニング：寛ぎを深める上質な空間
Living dining: This quality space is for relaxation and comfort.

Data
Title
Precious Style S90B-S type
Designer
Mami Mori
Area
85.26m²
Materials
Interior Wall :
　cloth
Interior Floor :
　marble, quince flooring

1	5
2	
3 4	6

1
ナチュラルな木目のデザインを活かしたワイドなアイランドカウンターキッチン
A wide island counter kitchen takes advantage of natural woodgrain design.

2
タワーならではの爽快な眺めを楽しみながら入浴できるビューバス
A bath with a grand view only available with towers.

3
大理石貼りの床が格調高い空間を演出する、シックな高級感に溢れるエントランス
Magnificent entrance with a chic and quality appearance featuring marble finished floor

4
パウダールーム：ダークブラウンの建具にグレーのカウンターが調和するシックな空間
Powder room: Dark brown furniture creates a harmony with a gray counter in this chic space.

5
ゆったりとした広さを確保した主寝室は、ダブルベッドを置いてもゆとりある空間
The expansive master bedroom is roomy enough to accommodate a double bed.

6
ウォークインクロゼットも完備した、フレキシブルに使える洋室
A western-style room secures flexibility in use, equipped with a walk-in closet.

The Kosugi Tower

スタンダードカラーの中に、オリエンタルな要素をミックス。スタンダードでありながらもトレンドを兼ね備えるため、さりげない和のエスプリやオリエンタルな雰囲気を取り入れたカラーテイスト。カリンの暖かいカラーの床材に、濃密で、赤味がかった木目調の建具がベーシックな落ち着きを醸し出す。モダンな家具のコーディネートにも似合う空間に仕上がっている

Oriental elements are mixed with standard colors. Though the overall texture is orthodox, a trendy look is also given; the taste in color incorporates an unimposing Japanese esprit and oriental atmosphere at the same time. A combination of warm-colored quince-wood flooring and thick and reddish woodgrain furniture gives a sense of belonging, comfort and peace. The space may well be coordinated with modern furniture.

バラッズ
Ballads S90D-SE type
Hitomi Beppu

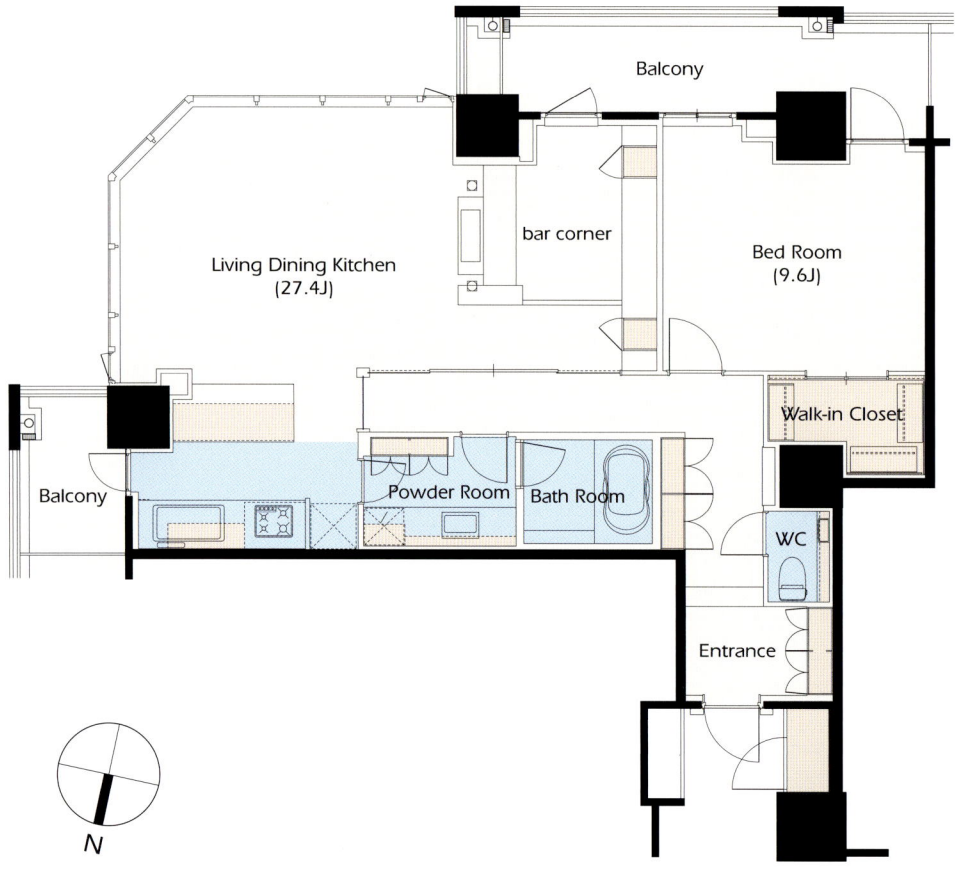

Data

Title
Ballads S90D-SE type

Designer
Hitomi Beppu

Area
90.00m²

Materials
Interior Wall :
  cloth
Interior Floor :
  marble, ebony pattern wood, carpet

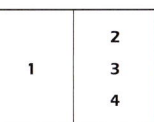

1
リビング・ダイニング：ヴィヴィッドな刺激に満ちた大人の世界観が漂う
Living dining: The room is filled with a sense of adult lifestyle in a vivid, fascinating and stimulating atmosphere.

2
広さ20帖のリビング・ダイニング。優雅な日常を感じるモード感あふれるライフステージ
This living dining room is as wide as 30 square meters. It is a stage for an elegant daily life with a "modal" sense.

3
夫婦やゲストとの優雅な語らいが楽しめるバーカウンターのあるダイニング
The dining room has a bar counter to enjoy elegant conversations with your one's partner or guests.

4
リビング：ブラックやダークグレーの色彩に、赤いアクセントカラーを効かせたモダンなインテリア
Living room: The modern interior is in black and dark gray colors accentuated with red.

1	
2	3
4	5

1
毛足の長い上質なカーペットを敷き詰めた、ひときわゴージャスな主寝室
The main bedroom appears especially gorgeous, covered with a quality carpet with long yarns.

2
モダンなデザインを追求し、イタリア製の4つ口コンロを搭載したオリジナルシステムキッチンを採用
In pursuit of a modern design adopted is a custom-designed system kitchen with an Italian four-burner kitchen stove.

3
システマティックに衣類を収納できるウォークインクロゼット
This walk in closet enables one to store clothes in a systematic manner.

4
ダークブラウンのスタイリッシュな空間にワイドな一面鏡が優雅に調和している
The stylish space in dark brown elegantly matches a wide full-length mirror.

5
人工大理石の浴槽と、石貼りの壁で贅沢な入浴感が楽しめるバスルーム
The bathroom with an artificial marble bathtub and stone-tiled walls enables one to enjoy a sense of luxury bathing.

ジャズのビートをイメージした、優雅でアンバーな世界観。「タワーライフとは、日常的利便性と、非日常的快適さを享受する喜びにある」という考えのもと、ONとOFFを巧みに切り替え、生活を洗練させるスタイルを提案。ブラックエボニー柄のデザインウッドの床材とヴェンゲ材の建具がしっとりとした背景を演出し、コルトレーンのバラードのようなビートを刻む

This elegant amber-based design is inspired by jazz beats. Following the concept that, "the essence of a life in the tower lies in an enjoyment of ordinary convenience and extraordinary comforts," a sophisticated and rhythmic lifestyle is proposed. Designed wood flooring in black ebony color and wenge-wood furniture sets a gentle background, cutting beats like a ballad by Coltrane.

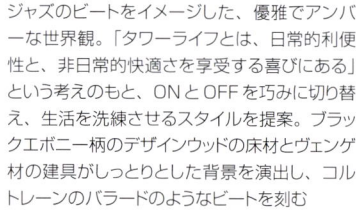

The Kosugi Tower

ザ・センター東京
The Center Tokyo

Nomura Real Estate Development Co., Ltd. / Mitsui Fudosan Co., Ltd. / Mitsubishi Estate Co., Ltd.
Fernando Vazquez / OBAYASHI CORPORATION

「ザ・センター東京」は360°東京を見晴らせる場所に位置する。この恵まれたロケーションの優位性を活かし、眺望重視の住戸プランを実現。それぞれの住まいの窓の外には、都内有数の庭園として知られる新宿御苑、緑豊かで広大な敷地に御用邸や御所、迎賓館がある赤坂御用地、山手線内で一番標高の高い箱根山がある戸山公園など、都心であることを忘れてしまいそうな緑のスポットの景観が広がっている。さらに高層ビルの姿も見渡せる東京の真ん中には、TOKYOのあらゆる美しい風景を我が物にする拠点でもある。街の景観と調和するフォーマルな外観デザインと、一歩中へ入るとタイを外してくつろぐ我が家への延長としての温かみ、親しみ、安らぎに満ちた共用空間の創造。その考えは、約6,000㎡の敷地に、贅沢ともいえるほどゆとりをもって配されたガーデンスペースにも生きている。都心にありながら、広大な緑をもつオーバルガーデンなど、どの空間も飾りではなく、日々の生活に潤いを与え、きちんと使いこなせるよう設計されている。

"The Center Tokyo" is located on the site with a 360-degree panorama of Tokyo. The unit design takes advantage of this favorable location, emphasizing the views from rooms. Outside the windows of each unit expands a view of the landscape spotted with parks and green areas including one of the best parks in Tokyo, the Shinjuku Gyoen National Garden, the expansion of the Akasaka Goyochi Palace accommodating Crown Prince Naruhito's palace, his residence and guesthouse, and the Toyama Park having the highest hill within the JR Yamanote Line, Mt. Hakone. Also having a command of view of skyscrapers, the site at the heart of Tokyo is an excellent base to call every beautiful scenery in the megalopolis one's own. The concept of creating a formal-looking exterior design that fits the townscape and public spaces filled with warmth, familiarity and comfort, where, once inside, one can remove one's tie and take a relax is also alive in the luxuriously wide garden of about 6,000 square meters. Though the site is in the city center, the design of buildings, interior spaces and site including an oval garden rich in green is not just for a decorative purpose but also to increase enjoyment in everyday life and to be fully functional.

Data

Title
THE CENTER TOKYO

Developer
Nomura Real Estate Development Co., Ltd.
Mitsui Fudosan Co., Ltd.
Mitsubishi Estate Co., Ltd.

Total Design Produce
Fernando Vazquez

Architect
OBAYASHI CORPORATION

Location
Shinjuku-ku, Tokyo

Site area
6,051.66㎡

Building area
2,899.35㎡

Total floor area
53,224.12㎡

Structure
RC

Completion
November, 2007

Materials
Exterior Wall :
  45x90tile, sprayed coating
  natural stone
Public Wall :
  natural stone, scratching paint
  non-combustible sliced venner
Public Floor :
  natural stone, carpet, flooring

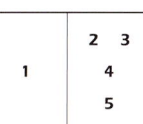

1

高さ約6.7mの重厚感ある黒御影石貼りの列柱の間を抜けていくメインエントランス。床と壁に自然の風合いが活かされた天然石を貼り詰め、天井までの大きなガラスを配している

One reaches the main entrance after passing through rows of massive 6.7-meter-high columns finished with black granite. Natural rock is applied to flooring and walls, taking advantage of natural texture characteristics while large glass panels are installed up to the ceiling.

2

大きな吹抜が広がるメインラウンジには、オーバルガーデンの木々の間から優しい陽光が射し込む

The main lounge with a spacious well is filled with gentle sunlight shining through trees in the oval garden.

3

オーバルガーデン全景：その一画には、ガラス張りのクラブハウスがあり、キッズルームと「キッチンスタジオ」を設置している

An overall view of the oval garden: A glass clubhouse with a kids' room and a "kitchen studio" is located in the garden.

4

滝が見渡せるカスケードラウンジ。和やかな表情のライムストーンの壁と天然石やカーペットの床によってエレガントな雰囲気に仕立てている

Cascade lounge with a view of the fall. The limestone walls with a sense of comfort and the floors covered with natural rock or carpet establish an elegant atmosphere.

5

パーティを愉しめるスカイラウンジ

In this sky lounge, one can even host parties.

180-Ap type
180-Ap type
Forward Style

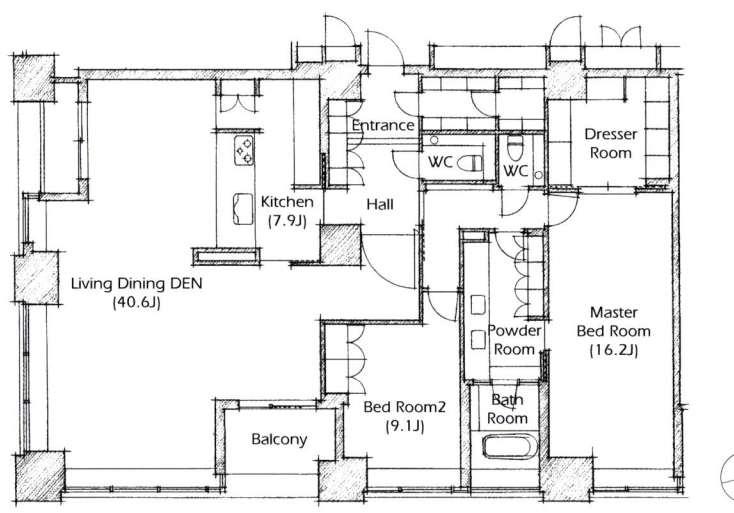

デザインのテーマは「日本の美意識を活かしたコンテンポラリーな住空間」
近年、欧米でも注目されている日本の伝統様式を取り入れたインテリア。このプランでも本物だけがもつ落ち着きと優しさ、五感に語り掛ける風合いをインテリアに反映している。贅沢に約175㎡もの広さを持ち、最上階ならではの眺望と東南角住戸ならではの開放感が享受できる空間は、豊かな人生を謳歌するにふさわしい、まさに邸宅と呼べるプラン。高い天井が創り出す広々とした室内と、そして細部にまで行き届いた上質感あふれるつくり、すべてにおいて極上の時間を提供している。

The design theme is "a contemporary living space taking advantage of a Japanese sense of beauty." An approach to interior incorporating the Japanese traditional style has attracted attention in the West. In this plan, the interior features comfort, gentleness and texture appealing to the five senses only found with something genuine. This luxurious unit has an area of as wide as about 175 square meters, and, positioned on the southeast corner of the top floor of the building offering a grand view and a sense of openness, the space is suitable for enjoying a rich, fulfilling life. The plan does the justice to the name of "mansions." Spacious rooms with a high ceiling and quality interior designs with attention given to every detail offer quality time.

Data
Title
180 Ap type
Designer
Forward Style
Area
175.98m²
Materials
Interior Wall :
 vinyl cloth
Interior Floor :
 natural stone, flooring

	2
1	3
	4

1
天井高2.88m～3.58mのリビング・ダイニングは、ハイサッシと折上天井によって空へと抜けるような開放感を演出
The ceiling height of living-dining rooms ranges from 2.88 to 3.58 meters. High sashes and the coved ceiling produce a sense of openness as if the room were in an open-air setting.

2
玄関ホールを抜けると、約40.6畳のリビング・ダイニング・DENが広がる。キッチンはこの開放感にふさわしいオープン型としている
When one passes through the entrance hall, one finds the living dining room and the den of about 60 square meters. To fit this expansion, an open kitchen is provided.

3
ダイニング・キッチンからリビングを臨む。気品のあるガラス製カップボードを置いたオープン型キッチンには、ダイニングとの間にパーティや朝食のひとときを優雅に愉しめる天然御影石のカウンターを配置
The living space seen from the dining kitchen. A natural granite counter that can elegantly be used for parties or breakfast is located between the open kitchen having an elegant glass cupboard and the dining space.

4
ゆとりを追求したマスターベッドルーム。床は英国産ウール100%の羊毛を使用したダークブラウンのカーペット
The master bedroom emphasizes roominess. The floor is covered with a dark brown carpet using 100% wool made in England

1
収納の高さを天井まで上げることによって、ゆとりある収納力を実現したドレッサールーム
The dresser room is equipped with storages up to the ceiling, ensuring the maximum storage capacity.

2
パノラマビューを愉しめるビューバスには、トップライト照明から優しい光が降り注ぐ
The view bath to enjoy a panoramic view of the city is gently filled with a light from the top light illumination.

3
ラボラトリー
Lavatory

4
パウダールーム：天然御影石のカウンタートップに2つのボールを備えたワイドな化粧洗面台を設置
The powder room has a wide two-sink washing stand with a natural granite countertop.

5
ベッドルーム
Bedroom

80-G type
80-G type
Forward Style

デザインのテーマは「家族が育む住まい」たとえば、子供が小さいうちは、子供部屋は主寝室と連結した空間に配している。そして成長に合わせて独立した居室へと移動。というふうに家族の触れ合いを大切にしながら、ライフスタイルの変化にも対応できる、ハイセンスであたたかく温もりのある空間。やわらかいインテリアカラーや、どの居室へも自然光をとりいれるよう配慮されている。

The design theme is "a residence that grows with a family." The kids' room is in a space linked to the master bedroom. When children start to grow, they will be moved to independent rooms. The stylish, warm and comfortable unit offers flexibility to correspond to lifestyle changes while attention is paid to a rich family life. Consideration is paid for making the color scheme of the interior gentle and taking natural light in every room.

Data

Title
80-G type
Designer
Forward Style
Area
83.08m²
Materials
Interior Wall :
vinyl cloth
Interior Floor :
natural stone, flooring

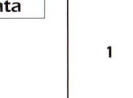

1
リビング：やさしいナチュラル系の色のフローリングが清潔感を醸し出す。またL型コーナーサッシから射し込む光が開放感を演出する
Living room: Natural colored flooring gives a sense of cleanliness. Lights from the L-shaped corner sash give a sense of openness.

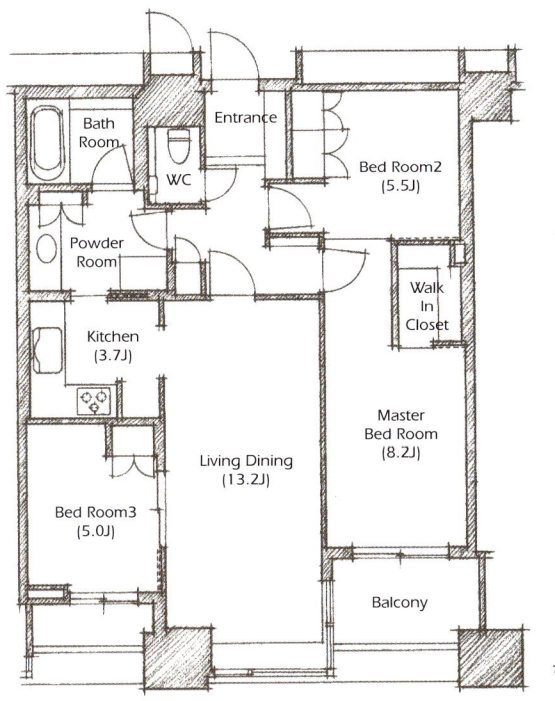

1
リビング・ダイニング：ホワイトオークの床材とウォールナットの建具という組み合わせで、輪郭をくっきり際立たせるようにデザインされている
Living-dining room: This combination of white oak flooring and walnut furniture is designed to emphasize the contours.

2
主寝室：奥の子供部屋との間に、さりげなく空間を隔てるウォークインクロゼットを配している
Master bedroom: A walk-in closet subtly separates the bedroom from the kids' room at the back.

3
機能性に定評のあるドイツ・ジーマティック社製の中でも、カウンタートップに天然御影石を、扉に突板を採用したグレード感あるシステムキッチン
Known for its functionality, this German SieMatic system kitchen has a natural granite countertop and sliced veneer doors, giving a sense of high quality.

ローレルタワー難波
Laurel Tower Namba
KINTETSU REAL ESTATE / KAJIMA DESIGN KANSAI

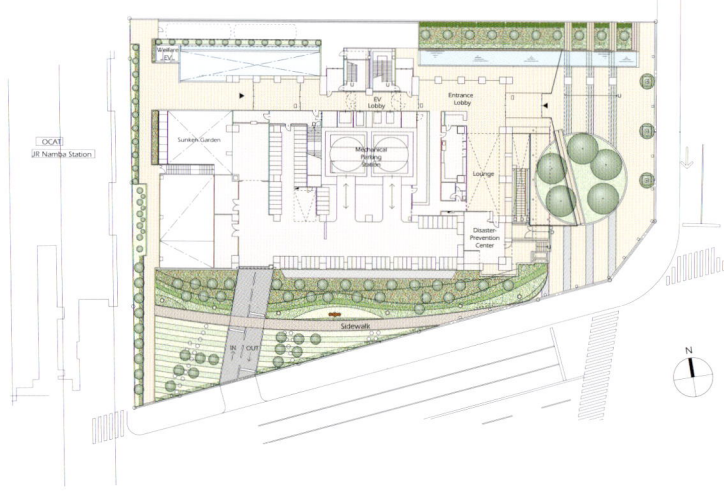

Data

Title
LAUREL TOWER NAMBA

Developer
KINTETSU REAL ESTATE

Architect
KAJIMA DESIGN KANSAI
(Toyoo Tsukada)

Location
Naniwa-ku, Osaka city

Site area
4,322.7m²

Building area
1,650.83m²

Total floor area
50,731.02m²

Area
50.12-143.10m²

Structure
RC (core wall-frame, duble tube double tube structure)

Completion
December, 2005

Materials
Exterior Wall :
  ceramic tile, aluminum panel
  aluminum louver, sprayed coating
Public Wall :
  diatomaceous earth, ceramiv tile
  scraching painting
Public Floor :
  ceramic tile, bamboo flooring
  tile carpet
Interior Wall :
  vinyl cloth
Interior Floor :
  decorated plywood composit flooring

Photo
Yoshiharu Matsumura

	2	3	4
1		5	
		6	

1
東側玄関ロビー前「鎮守の森」
"Chinju no mori" in front of the eastern entrance lobby

2
地上階エントランスとカスケード
The ground floor entrance and a cascading pool

3
南側「街角ギャラリー」
"Gallery on a Street Corner" to the south of the building

4
コモンズサロン:土壁画・黒田征太郎 作
Commons Salon whose mural paintings are by Seitaro Kuroda

5
地下玄関といぶし瓦タイルを使った壁泉アート
The subterranean entrance and the wall fountain using smoked tiles.

6
パーティールーム
Party room

1
2
3

1
寝室一体型のホテルライクな住戸
Hotel-like studio room

2
眺望抜群のフリープラン住戸
"Free design" residential unit with an excellent command of view

3
ゲストルーム(洋室タイプ)
Guestroom (Western style)

大阪中心部、通称「ミナミ」の繁華街の西に位置し、OCAT（大阪シティエアターミナル）内JR難波駅に直接、地下接続する超都心のタワー型マンションである。コンセプトは「アーバン―サトヤマ」。利便性のよい都心のスタイリッシュさに、里山のスローライフな住環境を融合させることを試行錯誤している。素材やモティーフのベースに考えたことは「土」。極端に田舎臭くなりすぎぬように、土の手触りや土から生み出される地層や褶曲、さらに湧き出る壁泉、そして熟成される鎮守の森、というストーリー・シーンを構成した。ロビーは黒田征太郎氏とのコラボレーションでざらざらの土壁を巨大な壁画アートとした。バルコニーファサードは横フィン形状のアルミルーバーを積層させ、上層ほどフィンを間引いている。サンクンガーデンの壁泉は「いぶし」瓦型タイルの順貼・逆貼による凹凸を利用して水流に不思議なパターンを生み出した。「鎮守の森」の大木クスノキはマウンドアップさせた直径15mのタマリュウ・サークルの中にそびえ立ち、身障者スロープの小道が森を突っ切っている。それぞれのシーンを住人のみならず街の人々も楽しめるところがこの建物最大の魅力である。時が経っても古ぼけない空間のポテンシャルを今、ようやくこの地に植え付けたばかりである。黒田征太郎氏の描く花の実をくわえ飛び立つ小鳥のように、人々が躍動する都市空間として、急がず熟成されていくことを信じたい。

To the west of the shopping quarters at the center of Osaka City, popularly known as "Minami", this city center tower condominium has direct underground access to the JR Namba Station in the Osaka City Air Terminal (OCAT). Its design concept is "Urban Satoyama (community forest.) It is a result of trial-and-error attempts to integrate stylish and convenient city life with a slow living environment found in satoyama. The approach to materials and motifs is based on "soil." While attention was paid to avoid making the scene too rustic, the conceptual design with an underlying story is prepared, featuring strata and folds suggested by the touch and use of soil, flowing wall mountains and "chinju no mori" (a luxuriant grove like that often found around the village shrine.) The granular mud walls of the lobby are turned into gigantic mural paintings through collaboration with Mr. Seitaro Kuroda. The facade of the balcony is made of layered horizontal-fin-shaped aluminum louvers. The number of fins gradually gets smaller for upper stories. The wall fountain in the sunken garden gives fantastic patterns of flow by taking advantage of projections and depressions of the smoked tiles alternately arranged in normal and reverse orientations. The tall camphor tree in the "chinju no mori" stands on the circular mound 15m in diameter and surrounded by Ophiopogon japonicus Gyokuryu, and a sloped path for physically handicapped runs across the circle. The biggest attraction of the building is the fact that each scene it offers can be enjoyed by both residents and people in town. An everlasting potential of the space has just been established. Like a bird having a seed in the beak and flying up drawn by Mr. Seitaro Kuroda, we hope that this space will grow and become mature to serve as an urban space to invigorate people.

クロスタワー大阪ベイ
X-Tower Osaka Bay

ORIX Real Estate Corporation / Mitsui Fudosan Co., Ltd. / Hankyu Realty Co.,Ltd.
agnès b. / SHOWA SEKKEI, INC.

「クロスタワー大阪ベイ」の外観デザインは、ニューヨーク・マンハッタン地区の摩天楼スタイル。それは超高層住宅にありがちな箱形の無表情な建物へのアンチテーゼであると同時に、超高層住宅としての品格と躍動する都市のランドマーク性を生み出すことを意図している。摩天楼スタイルであるアール・デコ、ネオ・ゴシック、アメリカン・ゴシックの共通モチーフである上昇感、高さの強調、垂直ラインの主張を、建物構造の核となるスーパーRCフレーム構法のスーパービームと柱の構成で表現。塔頂部・中間部・基壇部の三層構成による伝統的な建築デザインといった古典的建築様式の技法を取り入れてデザインされている。塔頂部は灯台をモチーフとし、建物をシンボリックに引き立たせてくれるクラウン（冠）。中間部は大理石風のタイルを山型に貼り分けて、伸びやかなフォルムを構成して、ステイタスを象徴的に魅せる。基壇部はライムストーン風の石貼りを主体として、コーニスやキーストーンといった古典的様式を採用し、建物の格調を高めている。さらに伝統的な正統派の建築デザインに加えて、土・空・緑・水を基調とした自然色のカラーコーディネートも外観デザインの大きな特徴。とくに、美しい摩天楼フォルムを創出するコーナーウィンドウには、海を意識したグリーニッシュブルーカラー（青緑色）の熱線吸収ガラスを採用されている。

The exterior design of the X-Tower Osaka Bay follows that of the skyscrapers in Manhattan, New York. It not only is an antithesis to a box-like, expressionless buildings often found with high-rise condominiums but also is intended to create a dignity as a ultra-high residential building and landmark in a vibrant city. In the design, a combination of columns and super beams of the Super RC Frame Method as the core of the building structure is taken advantage of to express the sense of ascension, emphasis on the height and highlights on vertical lines that are all common motifs of such skyscraper styles as Art Deco, Neo Gothic and American Gothic. Also utilized are methods of classic architectural styles, for example, the traditional design of tower, middle section and podium. The top of the building comparable to the tower is based on the concept of a lighthouse and serves as a crown to highlight the building in a symbolic manner. The middle section is covered with marble-like tiles forming shapes of mountains to constitute a flowing form, symbolizing a social status of living in this tower. The podium is mainly covered with limestone-like stone, employs cornices, keystones and other classical styles to enhance the dignity of the structure. In addition to the traditional, classical architectural design, the exterior design also features coordinated natural colors suggesting the earth, sky, greens and water. The corner windows to create the beautiful contours of the skyscraper especially employ greenish blue colored heat absorbing glass suggesting the color of the sea.

Data

Title
X-Tower Osaka Bay

Developer
ORIX Real Estate Corporation
Mitsui Fudosan Co., Ltd.
Hankyu Realty Co.,Ltd.

Public Space Design
agnès b.

Architect
SHOWA SEKKEI, INC.

Location
Minato-ku, Osaka city

Site area
5,568.41m²

Building area
residential building : 1,697.09 m²
commercial building : 2,112.64m²

Total floor area
residential building : 66,665.61m²
commercial building : 14,317.00m²

Structure
residential building : RC
commercial building : S (RC in part)

Completion
August, 2006

Materials
Exterior Wall :
 tile, stone, spray painting
Public Wall :
 painting

Materials
Public Floor :
 stone, carpet, tile
Interior Wall :
 vinyl cloth
Interior Floor :
 tile, flooring

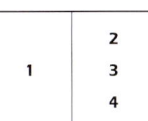

1

1階エントランス：フランスのファッションデザイナー・アニエスベー自身の手書き文字をデザインした天井部とあいまって、訪れる人をさりげなくエスコートする。

The first-floor entrance gently welcomes visitors, together with its ceiling arranged with handwritten letters by a French fashion designer, agnès b.

2

アニエスベーによる共用部デザイン。モロッコテイストをモダンアレンジした3層吹抜の大空間エントランスホール

The public section of the building is designed by agnès b. The large 3-story-high entrance hall represents a Moroccan taste arranged in a modern manner.

3

1階エントランスまわりを中心に、ウォーターテラス（水庭）を計画。ボードウォークをイメージした水際のデッキテラスや、桟橋のようなアプローチとあいまって、美しい波止場の雰囲気を創出している

A water terrace is designed around the entrance on the first floor. The deck terrace by the water inspiring a boardwalk and pier-like approaches all contribute to creating an atmosphere like a beautiful port.

4

モロッコの雰囲気を漂わせる2層吹抜のスカイラウンジ「シエルメール」

The 2-story-high sky lounge Ciel Mer has an atmosphere of Morocco.

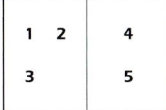

1
木枠に縁取られたアルコーブではアーティスティックな照明が慎ましく存在感を主張
In the wooden-framed alcove, artistic lighting modestly highlights its presence.

2
美意識が昇華されたエントランスホール。ふんだんに取り入れた天然石が威圧感を緩和する
The sense of beauty is condensed in the entrance hall. Amply used natural stones alleviate an air of coercion.

3
リビング・ダイニング・キッチン：観るものを魅了するパノラマビュー
The living room and the combined dining room-kitchen offers a panoramic view that attracts everyone's attention.

4
主寝室に付随したプライベートリビング。バーカウンターが設けられたくつろぎの空間
The private living space attached to the master bedroom offers a comfort with its bar counter.

5
主寝室：心地よい落ち着きがある伸びやかな空間
This spacious master bedroom is comfortable and relaxing.

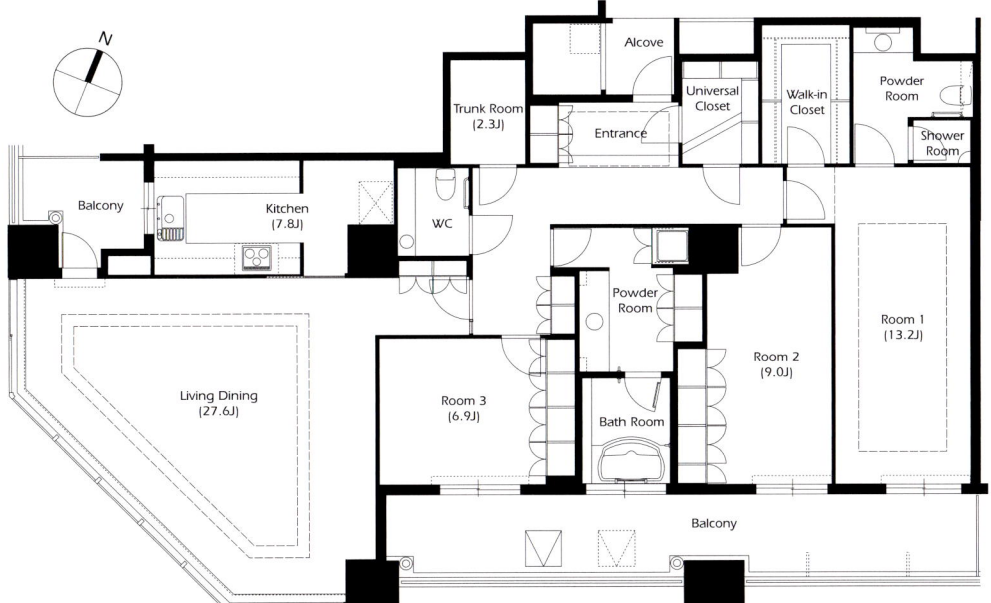

X-Tower Osaka Bay | 065

1
ワイドなアイランドカウンター
The wide island counter

2
インテリアとしても機能する美しいキッチン
This beautiful kitchen also serves as integrated part of the interior.

ザ・タワー大阪
The Tower Osaka

ORIX Real Estate Corporation / Mitsubishi Estate Co., Ltd. / Sumitomo Corporation
Kanden-Fudosan Co., Ltd. / Keihan Electric Railway Estate Co., Ltd.
Joint Venture of Takenaka Corporation and Mitsubishi Jisho Sekkei Inc.

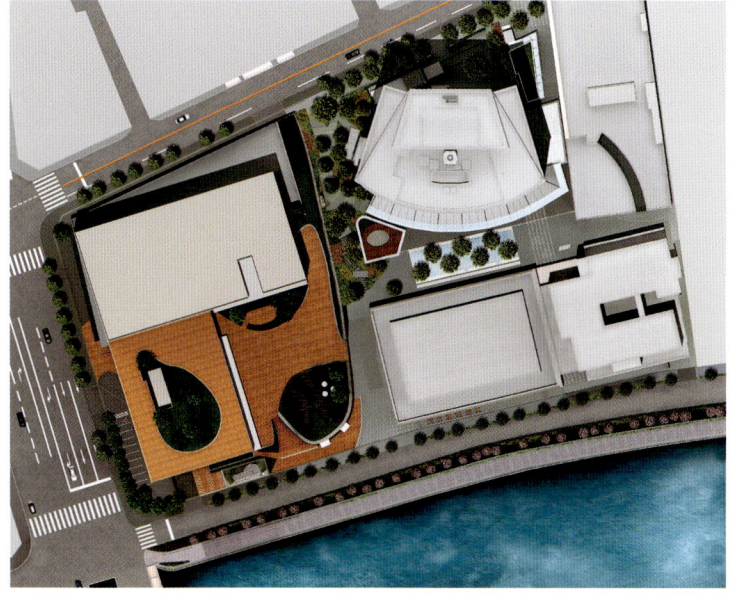

Data

Title
The Tower Osaka

Developer
ORIX Real Estate Corporation
Mitsubishi Estate Co., Ltd.
Sumitomo Corporation
Kanden-Fudosan Co., Ltd.
Keihan Electric Railway Estate Co., Ltd.

Architect
Joint Venture of Takenaka Corporation
and Mitsubishi Jisho Sekkei Inc.

Location
Fukushima-ku, Osaka city

Site area
5,697.13m²

Building area
2,660.51m²

Total floor area
73,206.15m²

Structure
RC

Completion
June, 2008

Materials
Exterior Wall :
natural stone, tile
Public Wall :
natural stone
Public Floor :
natural stone, carpet

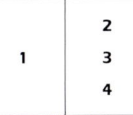

1
重厚な風格が漂うエントランスアプローチ。堂々と余裕を醸し出す風情にレジデンスライフのグレードの高さが象徴される
The approach to entrance has a massive elegance. Its magnificent and expansive atmosphere symbolizes the high-grade life in the residence.

2
レセプションロビー：2層吹抜で天井を曲線にデザインし、伸びやかな広がりを創出。片側には重厚な列柱と開放部を組み合わせ、自然光と緑の風景で演出
Reception lobby: Having a curved ceiling above the two-story well, the lobby is designed with a sense of spatial expansion. On one side are a row of massive columns and openings in between, highlighted by natural light and greens outside.

3
レセプションラウンジ：日常にラグジュアリーなゆとりの時間をもたらす開放的な共用スペース
Reception lounge: This open public space adds luxurious relaxing time to one's daily life.

4
レセプションサロン：レジデンスグレードを反映した格調高い社交スペースとなる集会室
Reception salon: This meeting room serves as a space for high-class social exchange reflecting the grade of the residence.

1
2
3

1
伸びやかなバルコニーに面して広がる、明るく安らぎに満ちた空間として設けたテラス
The terrace is established as a well lit, relaxing space facing an extensive balcony.

2
ビューラウンジと連動したバーラウンジ。しっとりと落ち着いた大人の時間を満喫できる
The bar lounge is linked to the view lounge. One can enjoy gentle and comfortable time for mature adults in there.

3
壮大な眺望と大いなる開放感を存分に活かすべく設計されたビューラウンジ。
The view lounge is designed to fully take advantage of a grand view and a great sense of freedom.

成熟した都市のさらなる進展には、衝撃とも言える独創性が必要だ。さまざまな特性のたぐい希なる集積を実現したこのプロジェクトは、そうした役割を担える複合機能都市。たとえば、高い文化発信力を持つ多目的ホールを設け、卓越した舞台芸術の提供の場としている。建物の意匠にもこだわり、バルセロナに立つガウディ設計のサグラダ・ファミリアのように人々の心を惹きつけるよう配慮。隣接地に一体開発されている朝日放送新社屋の影響も大きく、世界有数の情報拠点として発展したロンドンにも似て、最先端の情報が行き交う場ともなる。さらに、このプロジェクトの中心的建造物となる超高層タワーマンション「The Tower Osaka」は、エッフェル塔のように人々から特別の思い入れを寄せられるランドマークとしての存在感を主張する。今、日本はもとより、世界でも独創的な存在として異彩を放つ計画街区が、大阪の都心に新たな可能性を提示する。

For further development of a sophisticated city, a "shocking" originality is required. This project is a unique accumulation of various features and characteristics, creating "a city in a city" with complex functions. For example, a multi-purpose hall highly capable of dispatching cultural information is established to serve as a place to offer theatrical arts of excellence. The design of the buildings is also carefully crafted. Like Sagrada Familia in Barcelona designed by Gaudi, charms to attract people's attention are given to every structure. The presence of the new building of Asahi Broadcasting Corporation under development at the same time in the adjacent site is also influential, and the site of the project will be a place where latest information is exchanged like in London that has been developed as one of the most important information bases in the world. The high-rise tower condominium to become the core structure of this project, "The Tower Osaka" will ensure its presence as the landmark to which people are deeply attached to like the Eiffel Tower. This extraordinary block conspicuous not only in Japan but also in the world will present a new potential at the heart of Osaka City.

ゴージャスエレガンス
Gorgeous Elegance
Hiroko Ashihara

1

リビング・ダイニング：上品な折上天井も設け、空間の格調を高めている。

Living-dining room: The room has an elegant coved ceiling increasing a sense of refinement of the space.

豊かな時間を過ごすことができ、その先に豊かな人生が訪れるような住空間を目指してプランニングされている。nLDKという従来の間取りにとらわれず、フレキシブルな発想で空間の隅々にまで充実したライフシーンが広がるよう配慮。超高層ペントハウスとしての誇り高いグレードにもこだわり、ラグジュアリーなインテリアテイストで満たしたほか、街の景色を全居室から眺められるよう設計。さらに、一戸建てのような着地感が得られるよう、スカイテラスをはじめとする特徴的な仕様も多彩に採用。揺るぎないステイタスを確固たるものとしたエグゼクティブミドルにふさわしい、誇らしく、しかもスタイリッシュな邸宅感を実現している。

The unit is planned to offer a living space where one can enjoy rich and relaxing time to lead to a life of fulfillment. Without being restricted by the conventional layout of n-LDK, consideration is paid to every corner of the unit with a flexible viewpoint. To serve as a high-grade, penthouse-like unit in a high-rise tower, the interior of each residential unit is finished with a luxurious taste, and all the rooms are designed to overlook the city. In addition, to give a sense of closeness to the ground as if it were a detached house, a sky terrace and other unique specifications are fully implemented. Each unit gives its owner a sense of pride and a feeling of living in a stylish residence appropriate for a middle-aged executive with an established status.

Data

Title
  Gorgeous Elegance
Designer / Architect
  Hiroko Ashihara
Area
  232.92m²
Materials
  Interior Wall :
    marble, cloth
  Interior Floor :
    marble, flooring, carpet

1
趣深い和の風情に包まれて過ごせる書斎と、日本間伝統の床の間と炉を備えた本格仕様の茶室
The study in a cultivated Japanese taste and the fully equipped tearoom with the recess in which a scroll is hung and a fire pot.

2
爽やかで楽しいクッキングシーンを演出する、開放感にあふれインテリア性にも優れたキッチン
The open kitchen having an excellent interior design enables one to enjoy comfortable cooking.

3
迎賓仕様にこだわった格調高いエントランス
Every detail of the elegant entrance hall is to welcome guests.

4
心静かに安らぎながら優雅なひとときを過ごせる、ゆとりと品位に満たされた主寝室
The master bedroom gives a sense of comfort and high grade, enabling one to relax and enjoy elegant time.

5
快適性に優れ広々としたトイレ
A wide and comfortable lavatory

1
ガラス張りの引き戸を採用した洗面化粧室。2ボウルタイプのワイドな洗面化粧台には重厚な天然石仕様のカウンタートップを採用し、格調高い雰囲気を醸している
The dressing room has glass-plated sliding door. A wide dresser with two sinks has a massive, native-rock countertop, giving a stylish atmosphere.

2
バスルーム：壁面の色調をツートーンとし、落ち着いた雰囲気を演出
Bathroom: The wall is in two-tone giving a quiet atmosphere.

3
バスルームから洗面化粧室を臨む
Dressing room seen from the bathroom

Park City Musashikosugi

パークシティ武蔵小杉
Park City Musashikosugi

Mitsui Fudosan Co., Ltd. / NIPPON OIL REAL ESTATE CO.,LTD. / Jun Mitsui / Turan Duda
Toshiaki Yanagida(GREEN AND ARTS Co.,LTD.) / Takenaka Corporation

1
商業施設棟を足元にひかえるステーションフォレストタワー（右）、公共公益施設を抱くミッドスカイタワー（左）
The Station Forest Tower (left) has commercial facilities at the foot of the tower while the Mid Sky Tower (right) is adjacent to public facilities.

Data

Title
Park City Musashikosugi

Developer
Mitsui Fudosan Co., Ltd.
NIPPON OIL REAL ESTATE CO.,LTD.

Basic Plan
Jun Mitsui

Facade Design
Turan Duda

Landscape Design
Toshiaki Yanagida
(GREEN AND ARTS Co.,LTD.)

Architect
Takenaka Corporation

Location
Kawasaki city, Kanagawa

Site area
23,640.35m²
station forest tower : 8,222.82m²

Building area
station forest tower : 2,005.84m²

Total floor area
station forest tower : 80,998.33m²

Structure
RC (SRC in part)

Completion
October, 2008

Materials
Exterior Wall :
50x100tile, granite
Public Wall :
granite, vinyl cloth
Public Floor :
granite, tile carpet, flooring

1	
2	
3	

1

ベンチや東屋のある憩いのスペース。ミッドスカイタワーの敷地内に設けられた「ふれあいの丘」

This relaxing space has benches and a kiosk. It is called the Fureai no Oka (Hill for Exchanges) on the site of the Mid Sky Tower.

2

東急東横線「武蔵小杉」駅前の顔にふさわしいオープンスペース、ミッドスカイタワーに設けられた「波紋の広場」

This public space is ideal for the station front of the Musashikosugi Station of the Tokyu Toyoko Line and is called "Hamon no Hiroba" (Hill of Waves) on the site of the Mid Sky tower.

3

メインエントランス：テクスチャー、カラーリング、デザインへのこだわりによって気品と風格を映し出すとともに、ガラスの向こうに緑が広がり、森の中のやすらぎを感じさせる

Main Entrance: While careful considerations to the texture, coloring and design gives a sense of elegance and dignity, green trees beyond the glass walls reminds one of relaxation in the forest.

1	2
	3
	4

1

ステーションフォレストタワーロビーラウンジ：「やすらぎの泉」を眺められる開放的な空間

Lobby Lounge of the Station Forest Tower: One can see "Yasuragi no Izumi" (Spring of Comfort) from this space with a sense of openness.

2

色とりどりのハーブと、パーゴラを設けたミッドスカイタワーハーブガーデン

Colorful herbs are planted and pergolas are installed in the herb garden at the Mid Sky Tower.

3

ステーションフォレストタワーシティラウンジ：2層吹抜を活かした大きなガラスウォールの先には、東京の風景が広がる

City Lounge of the Station Forest Tower: A view of Tokyo extends in all direction beyond the large glass-walls taking advantage of the 2-story well.

4

2棟の屋上に設けられた、空を肌で感じる空間「スカイテラス」。ガラスウォールに囲まれ、ウッドデッキで仕上げられた開放感が満ちている

Sky Terraces are established at the roofs of the two towers, enabling one to directly feel the expansion of the sky. A sense of openness is provided by the surrounding glass-walls and wood deck finish.

住む、育む、大空へはばたく。このプロジェクトには2羽の鳥に例えた「ツインバード」をコンセプトに様々な思いが込められている。まず、2つのタワーが共鳴しあう計画とし、ツインとしての存在感を追求。建物のフォルムは、上層部にゆるやかな曲線を用いて、翼を広げる二羽の鳥を表現している。またシンボリックな頂部デザインの構成等、地上47階・59階建ての超高層ランドマークとして、角度によって異なる見え方を基本とし、個性あふれる「遠景」となることをめざした。「パークシティ武蔵小杉」のファサードは、タワー上部の曲線を反復し、上から下へ斜めに流れるようなラインを構成し、新しい都市が誕生する躍動感を表すものとしてデザインされている。この流麗な表現は、超高層建築としての鋭さを軽減するとともに、自然の調和をイメージさせる表情を創出させている。また、バルコニーの陰影など横線の強調により、直線と曲線、そして縦と横という対比するファクターの競演をめざしている。そして、ファサードを構成するもうひとつの大きな特徴として挙げられるのが、バルコニー部分におけるガラス素材の採用。これは外観としての透明感、住空間からつながるタワーライフの開放感、眺望の確保などに配慮するとともに、角度によって異なる見え方を生み出す工夫でもある。つまり、太陽の光によってバルコニーのガラスが反射を生み出し、様々な表情を創出する。また、外観カラーは、多摩川など豊かな自然をイメージさせるニュートラルなカラーをベースに、鳥の羽根をモチーフとした鮮やかな色彩を用いてデザイン構成されている。

To live, nurture and fly into the sky. In the concept of this project, the two towers are compared to a couple of birds. First, the towers are planned to establish permanent presence as a pair. The upper stories form gentle curves to express two birds spreading their wings. As high-rise landmarks of 47 and 59 stories above ground respectively, the buildings including their symbolically designed tops are designed in a way that they should show different forms as backgrounds in the landscape, depending on where it is viewed from. The facade of Park City Musashikosugi reproduces the curving lines at the top of the tower as appropriate, constitutes a gently sloping lines from top to bottom and is designed to represent a sense of energy when a new town is created. This elegant expression reduces a sense of prominence and gives an impression of harmony with nature. Further, emphasis on the shades of balconies and other horizontal lines results in impressive contrasts of straight and curving lines, vertical and horizontal lines, and other opposing factors. Another key feature of the facade is employment of glass materials for the balconies. While this approach contributes to a sense of transparency as part of the exterior, a sense of openness from the interior residential spaces and secured command of view, it also helps the buildings to appear differently when seen from different angles. In other words, sunlight is reflected on the glass surfaces of the balconies, giving a wide variety of expressions. The colors of the exterior are based on neutral ones suggesting the Tama River and other rich nature and outlined by vivid colors whose motifs are taken from birds' feathers.

M55D
M55D

1
リビング・ダイニング・寝室。琉球畳を設え、趣のある空間に仕上げている
Living and dining space and bedroom: Covered with Ryukyu tatami mats, the space gives a certain charm.

2
リビングからマスターベッドルームを臨む
The master bedroom seen from the living space.

Data
Title
　M55D
Area
　54.62m²
Materials
　Interior Wall :
　　vinyl cloth
　Interior Floor :
　　Ryukyu-Tatami, flooring

M90C
M90C

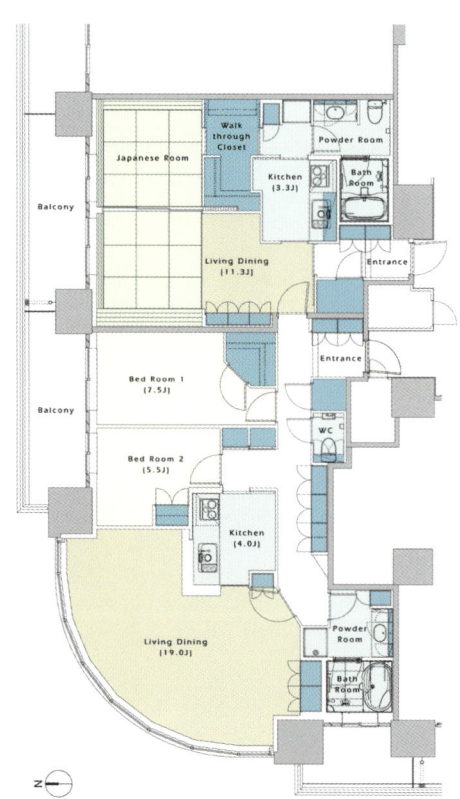

M55D + M90C
二世帯近居プラン
plans for two families living in neighborhood

Data

Title
M90C

Area
88.88m²

Materials
Interior Wall :
vinyl cloth
Interior Floor :
granite, cherry flooring

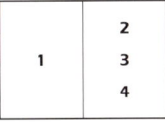

1
リビング・ダイニングを臨む
Living and dining space seen from the outside

2
開放感のあるリビング・ダイニング。全体の印象を引き締めるアクセントとして、床と天井に木目を強調したチェリーをカラーセレクト
Living and dining space gives a sense of expansion. Cherry wood with highlighted wood grain is used for the floor and ceiling to give an accent on the total impression.

3
リビングルームからの夜景
A night view from the living room

4
ゆとりのあるマスターベッドルーム。フローリングや建具にチェリー材を採用し、上質で落ち着きの感じられる空間
The spacious master bedroom. Cherry is employed for flooring and furniture, giving a sense of quality and comfort.

M90F
M90F

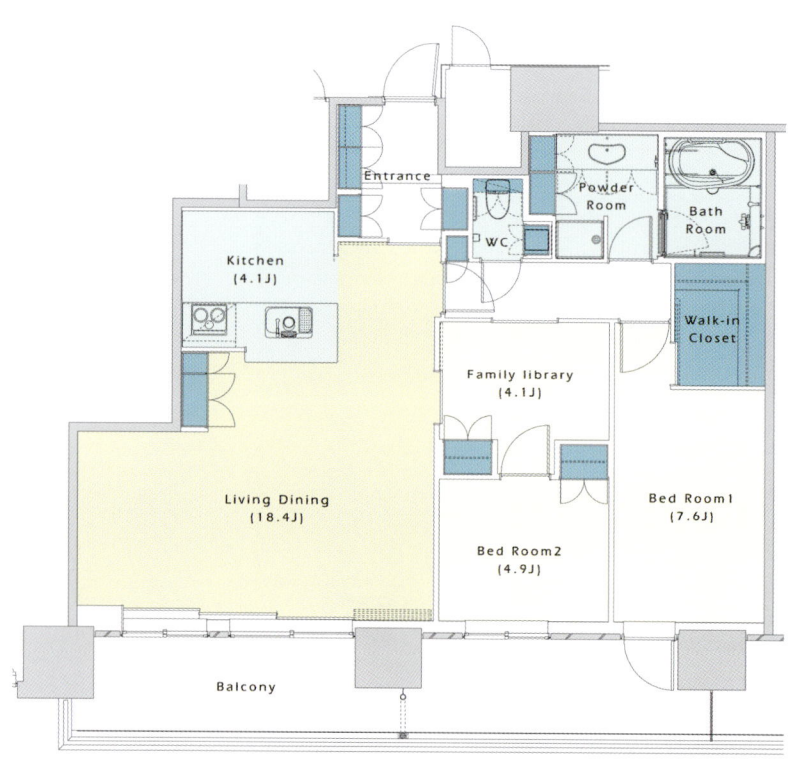

Data

Title
M90F

Area
89.00m²

Materials
Interior Wall :
  vinyl cloth
Interior Floor :
  marble, Walnut flooring

	2	3
1	4	5

1

リビング・ダイニング：リゾートホテルのようなくつろぎ。大理石の床とウォールナットをコーディネートした自然の温もりを演出

This living-dining space offers a sense of relaxation as if one were in a guestroom of a resort hotel. A combination of marble flooring and walnut furniture lets one feel warmth of nature.

2

機能も充実したインテリア性のあるキッチン

Fully equipped kitchen is also excellently designed as part of the interior.

3

エントランスホールからリビングを臨む。リビングまで敷き詰められた大理石やウォールナットの建具など、空間に一体感を生んでいる

The living room seen from the entrance hall. The marble-covered corridor leading up to the living room as well as the walnut furniture creates a sense of integrity in the space.

4

ファミリールーム：書斎、デスク、パソコンをしつらえ、家族が自然と集う知的な空間

Family room: Equipped with bookshelves, desks and a PC, this space with a sense of intelligence naturally attracts member of the family.

5

パウダールーム

Powder room

1
2

1

ウォールナットのフローリングを採用し、あたたかみのあるマスターベッドルーム

The master bedroom employs walnut flooring that gives warmth to the space.

2

洋室からファミリールームを臨む

Family room seen from the Western-style room

ミッドサザン・レジデンス御殿山
Mid Southern Residence Gotenyama

Mitsubishi Estate Co., Ltd. / Sojitz Corporation / Tokyo Tatemono Co., Ltd.
Mitsubishi Jisho Sekkei Inc.

目黒川を渡ると現れる、小さな森。御殿山の街並みが持つ落ち着きと、その森は不思議なほどに親和している。木々にろ過された光の中を過ぎ、静かな鏡面が映し出す木立を眺める。様々な場面で自然の要素を感じられるアプローチの創出。緑と水、光の波長が絡み合って生み出される景観や空間は、単に憩いや安らぎだけでなく、私たちを取り巻く環境の存在を認識させてくれる。江戸時代から桜の名所として知られる御殿山の春には、多くの人々が訪れたという。そうした歴史も踏まえ、季節の移ろいを楽しむ日本特有の文化性を活かすべく、四季を意識した樹木構成としている。高層タワー・マンションにおける緑が作り出す景観は、都市環境やそこに住む人の生活にとって重要な意味をもっている。エントランスを抜けての外出や帰宅時、緑と水のアプローチであるトランジショナル（遷移）・ゾーンは気持ちの切り替えに欠かせない。春の桜、夏の緑陰、秋の紅葉。一年を通して低木や地被類の緑が周囲を覆う。そんなヒューマンスケールを大切にした森が、東京ミッドサザンの新しいオアシスとなる。

Across the Meguro River, one sees a small forest. The woods somehow match the quiet townscape of Gotenyama. Passing through lights filtered by the trees, one can see a cluster of trees reflected upon water. Created is an approach with natural elements in different scenes. Green, water and waves of light are entwined with each other, generating a landscape and a space that gives us not only a rest and comfort but also a recognition of the presence of the environment around us. Well-known as a place for beautiful cherry blossoms, Gotenyama has attracted many people in spring since the Edo Era. Taking this history into consideration, the tree composition is designed in conscious of the four seasons by taking advantage of the cultural uniqueness of the Japanese to enjoy change of the seasons. The landscape created by the green spaces around the high-rise residential tower has an important meaning for the urban environment as well as the quality of life of the residents. When one goes out or comes back home through the entrance, the transitional zone on the approach with trees, plants and water is indispensable for a change in attitude. Cherry trees in spring, shades under trees in summer, and red leaves in autumn. Throughout the year, shrubs and ground covers surround the site. The forest on a human scale will serve as the new oasis in the Mid-Southern Residence.

Data

Title
Mid Southern Residence Gotenyama

Developer
Mitsubishi Estate Co., Ltd.
Sojitz Corporation
Tokyo Tatemono Co., Ltd.

Architect
Mitsubishi Jisho Sekkei Inc.

Location
Shinagawa-ku, Tokyo

Site area
4,825.00m²

Building area
1,818.80m²

Total floor area
24,446.77m²

Structure
RC

Completion
March, 2007

Materials
Exterior Wall :
  45x90ceramic tile, natural stone sprayed coating
Public Wall :
  natural stone, aluminum, paint
Public Floor :
  natural stone

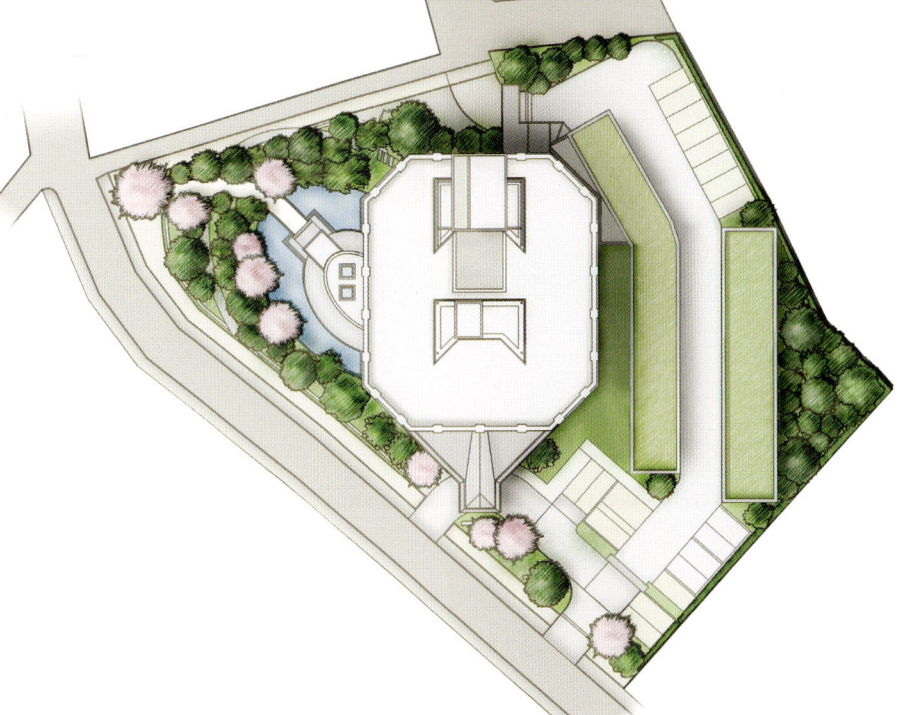

	2	3
1	4	
	5	

1
タワーへと続く緑と一体化したアプローチは、歩みを進めるごとに変化する緑の表情を、心ゆくまで感じられる。やがて辿り着くのは水盤「クレッセントウォーター」。その奥に「メインエントランス」と「オーバルホール」が浮かび上がる
The approach to the tower integrated with the green changes its face with every step one takes, enabling one to fully enjoy its expressions. One finally reaches the pool, Crescent Water, reflecting the main entrance and the Oval Hall behind it.

2
色彩と素材感あふれたエントランスロビー。オーバルホールとは対照的に彩りや温もりを感じさせる吹き抜けの空間
The entrance lobby is rich in colors and textures of materials. In contrast with the Oval Hall, this space in a well impresses one with lush colors and a sense of warmth.

3
敷地配置図
Site plan

4
アプローチから館内へ入ると、白で統一された清潔感あふれる楕円の空間・オーバルホールが広がる。一面のガラス窓からまばゆいほどの光が射し込み、森の気配と水面のゆらめきを感じられる
When one enters the building through the approach, one will find oneself in a clean, oval-shaped space in white or the Oval Hall. In effulgent light through the glass walls, one feels as if one were in the woods with a rippling pond.

5
ビューラウンジ：キッチンカウンターを備えた大人のためのBARのような空間からアーバンビューを一望できる
View lounge: This bar-like space with a kitchen counter for adults offers a panoramic view of the city.

Mid Southern Residence Gotenyama

CALM GENTLE Oriental Modern Taste
CALM GENTLE Oriental Modern Taste
Kunikazu Takatori

タイやバリのリゾートに見られる無垢の木のインテリアをイメージし、オリエンタルテイストにモダンな感覚を加えた落ち着きにあふれる住空間。独特な味わいのあるカリン材のフローリング、重厚感のある天然木を随所に用いた建具など、素材そのものの肌合いを大切にした空間

Inspired by the interior made of solid natural wood often seen in Thai and Bali resorts, this comfortable residential space has an oriental taste with a modern concept added. Textures of materials are fully exploited including quince flooring and fixtures of massive natural wood.

Data
Title
  CALM GENTLE Oriental Modern Taste
Designer
  Kunikazu Takatori
Area
  100m²
Materials
  Interior Wall :
   painting
  Interior Floor :
   natural stone, flooring

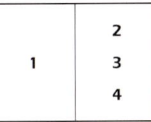

1
リビング・ダイニング・キッチン：ワイドウィンドウの窓辺にカウンターを設け、視線を窓辺に誘導する仕掛けとしている

The living room and a dining room-cum-kitchen has a counter by the wide windows to naturally guide one's line of sight to the view from them.

2
ディスプレイシェルフが設けられたリビング・ダイニング。目を和ませるフローリングと左官仕上げの壁は外装材と変わらぬ趣を醸成している

The living and dining space features wall-mounted display shelves. The flooring kind to the eyes and plaster-finished walls create a sophisticated atmosphere in common with the exterior materials.

3
自然の素材が持つ風合いが感じられるダイニング・キッチン

The kitchen with a dining area offers one with a feeling of natural materials.

4
シックな雰囲気で心からくつろげるマスターベッドルーム

The master bedroom has a chic and elegant atmosphere for ultimate relaxation.

Mid Southern Residence Gotenyama

1	
2	
3	4

1
穏やかな心地よさがあるベッドルーム
The bedroom gives a gentle and comfortable impression.

2
ドレッシングルーム:カウンターや床・壁に御影石を用いて上質な雰囲気に浸れる
The dressing room uses granite for its counter, floor and walls, giving a sense of quality.

3
ガラスの扉や御影石をふんだんに用いたホテルライクなバスルーム
The hotel-like bathroom amply employs glass doors and granite.

4
ラボラトリー
Lavatory

GRACEFUL MATTE
GRACEFUL MATTE
Yumi Hasumi (Mec Design International Corporation)

1

1
リビング・ダイニング：都市の「動」と「静」を愉しむ洗練の空間

The living and dining area is a sophisticated space to enjoy "animation" and "stillness" of the city.

都市生活においてプライベートな時間を大切にした癒しの空間として、素材の持ち味が愉しめるMATTE（ツヤ消し）のインテリアテイストで統一されている。自然の風合いを生かしたフローリングと、ダークブラウンの建具とのコントラストが醸し出す洗練。やすらぎとともに、落ち着いた空間が生まれている。

For this healing space for private hours in urban living, the entire interior has a consistent style of matte to take advantage of distinctive quality of materials. The contrast between the flooring utilizing natural feeling and fixings in dark brown leads to sophistication. The space gives a sense of healing and comfort.

Data

Title
GRACEFUL MATTE

Designer
Yumi Hasumi
(Mec Design International Corporation)

Area
70m²

Materials
Interior Wall :
vinyle cloth
Interior Floor :
natural stone, flooring

1	2
3	
4	

1
自然の風合いが感じられる落ち着いたエントランスホール
A feeling of nature lingers in the quiet entrance hall.

2
キッチン：木目を抑えた扉材とクリア塗装のフローリングの対比でシックな雰囲気を増し、優しさと温もりが感じられる
The kitchen gives a chic atmosphere augmented by the contrast between the doors with modest wood grains and the floor with clear coating, giving a sense of gentleness and warmth.

3
リビングと什器で仕切られた書斎スペース
The study is separated from the living room by the furniture.

4
ホテルのようなしっとりとした空気感を意識したマスターベッドルーム
The master bedroom has an agreeable air like in a hotel.

ローレルタワーサンクタス梅田
Laurel Tower Sanctus Umeda
KINTETSU Real Estate CO., LTD. / ORIX Real Estate Corporation
Takenaka Corporation

1
メインエントランス：ホテル感覚のカーエントランスを設置している
Main entrance: Hotel-like car entrance is provided.

2
敷地配置図
Site Plan

3
水と緑のランドプラン「アクアフォレスト」。円を描くように配した水盤とそれを囲む緑のマウンドは、「都心に出現した泉」イメージしている
Aqua Forest, a land plan based on water and plants. The pool designed to form a semi-circle and green mounds surrounding them inspires a "spring that has emerged at the heart of the city."

4
ホテルのロビーを思わせる高級感あふれるエントランスホール。2層吹抜の開放感と淡い間接照明で演出されている
The entrance hall suggests the lobby of a superior-grade hotel, contributed by the spaciousness in the two-story well and soft, indirect lighting.

5
豊かな眺めが優雅なひと時を演出するオーナーズラウンジ
The owner's lounge with a grand view provides stylish, elegant time,

1	3
	4
2	5

Data

Title
Laurel Tower Sanctus Umeda

Developer
KINTETSU Real Estate CO., LTD.
ORIX Real Estate Corporation

Architect
Takenaka Corporation

Location
Kita-ku, Osaka city

Site area
2,500.04m²

Building area
1,134.37m²

Total floor area
31,925.82m²

Structure
RC

Completion
February, 2007

Materials
Exterior Wall :
 natural stone, 45x95 ceramic tile
Public Wall :
 tile, vinyl cloth
Public Floor :
 tile, tile carpet

「ローレルタワーサンクタス梅田」は地上44階建ての超高層タワー。約143mのその姿は、やはりこの街の、新しいランドマークとして、人々の視線を集める存在となるだろう。超高層建築物を創ることは、都市に新たな景観を創造することでもある。その大きな使命を果たすために、都心に、そしてこの街にふさわしい建築物のあり方を追求し、そのタワーフォルムや外壁素材にこだわっている。外観のデザインコンセプトは、「やさしく都市景観に溶け込む」超高層タワー。基壇部は、重厚で都会的な印象を演出するグレーの天然石を採用。また、建物はアースカラータイルの濃淡で縦ラインを強調し、横連窓のサッシによる連続で横ラインを構成。また、頭頂部は全面ガラスとし、スカイラインの軽快さを演出している。そして、建物を可能な限りセットバックさせ、敷地の北側には広々とした公開空地「アクアフォレスト」を確保。多彩な緑を植え込み、緑豊かな空間を演出している。「都心のオアシス」と呼ぶにふさわしいやさしさが、超高層の足元をやさしく包み込む。

Laurel Tower Sanctus Umeda is a super high-rise tower of about 143 meters and will naturally be the new landmark of this town, attracting people's interest. Creating a high-rise architecture means creating a new landscape in town. To accomplish this important mission, the way of the building to be at the heart of the town in this particular city is pursued, paying close attention to its form and exterior wall materials as a tower. The design concept of the exterior is a high-rise tower "to softly melt into the urban landscape." Gray natural stone is employed for the podium section in order to produce a sophisticated urban impression with a sense of dignity. The vertical lines of the building are highlighted, using different shading of earth color tiles while sashes of the series of windows in the horizontal direction constitute horizontal lines. The crown of the tower is fully glass-enclosed to give a light and streamlined impression of the skyline. The building is set back as much as possible to secure a wide public open space, Aqua Forest, to the north of the site. Different green trees and plants are arranged for creating a space rich in green. The gentleness suitable for the name of the "oasis in the city" softly surrounds the foot of the tower.

De type
De type
Wacoal Corp.

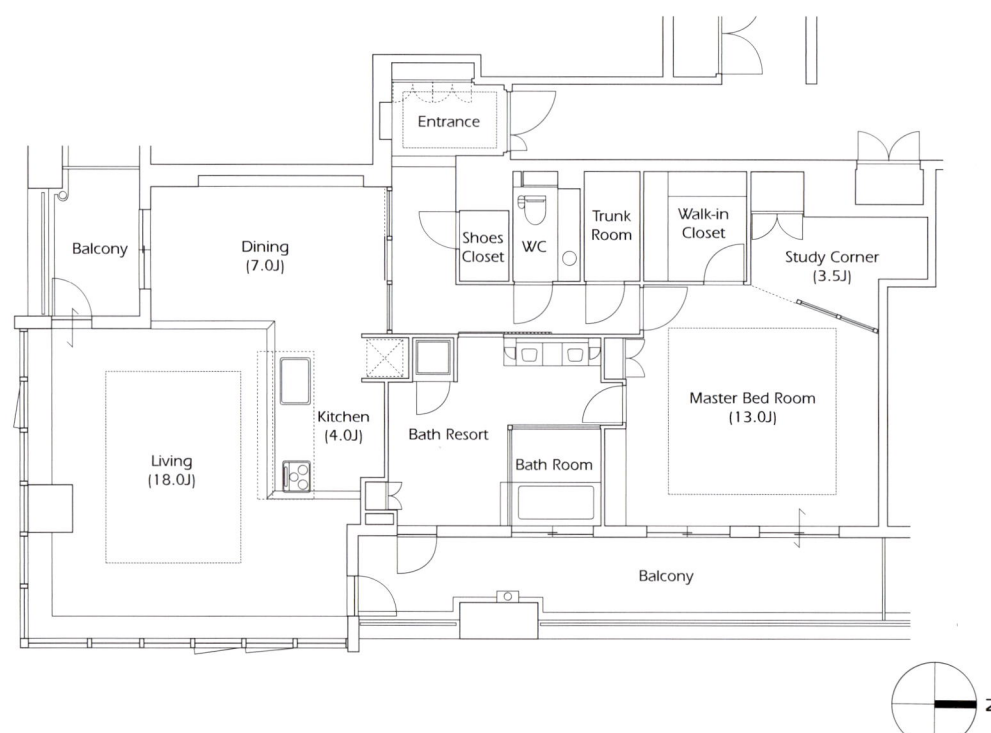

Data

Title
De type

Designer
Wacoal Corp

Area
120.69m²

Materials
Interior Wall :
vinyl cloth
Interior Floor :
natural stone, flooring, carpet

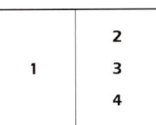

1

リビングからキッチンを臨む。超高層タワーライフにふさわしい「ゆとり」を感じる落ち着いた空間

The kitchen seen from the living area. This relaxing space gives a sense of "comfort" appropriate for a life in the high-rise tower.

2

廊下からダイニングを臨む。光の演出、影の演出が生むコントラストが、時には物静かに、時には饒舌にその姿を変える

Dining area seen from the corridor. The contrast between the carefully designed light and shade reveals different faces of the area over time.

3

リビング・ダイニング・キッチン：大きな窓からひろがる眺望が住空間に更なる開放感を演出している

Living room and a dining room-cum-kitchen: A view beyond a large window adds a sense of further spaciousness to the living space.

4

開放感あるアイランドキッチン。「加える」より「捨てる」という発想で凝らされた意匠が、透明感すら感じさせる

Island kitchen with a sense of openness. The design based on the idea of "discarding" rather than "adding" contributing to an impression of simplicity and transparency.

1
天然大理石を採用した玄関ホール・廊下
Entrance hall and corridor with natural marble

2
ゆるやかな時間に満ちた主寝室。奥には書斎コーナー付随している
The master bedroom is filled with slow time. A study corner is also established at the back of the room.

3
窓外に広がる夜景を楽しみながらリラックスできるバスリゾート
The bath resort enables one to relax oneself while enjoying a night view of the city outside the window.

Be type
Be type
Wacoal Corp.

1

1
まるで都心の空を切りとるようにして、その心地よさをリビングルームへといざなうパノラマウィンドウ

The panorama windows cut off the sky of the city to be part of the living room.

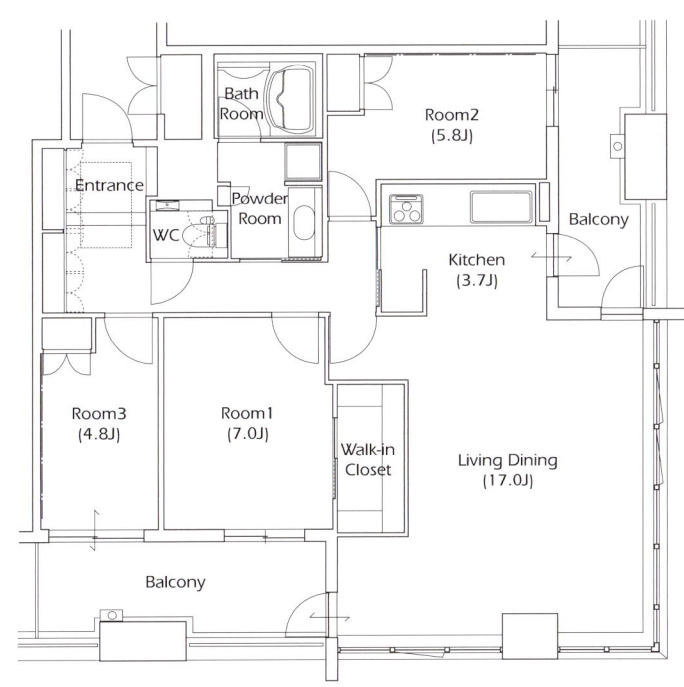

Data
Title
  Be type
Designer
  Wacoal Corp.
Area
  91.85m²
Materials
  Interior Wall :
    vinyl cloth
  Interior Floor :
    marble, flooring, carpet

1
落ち着きのある雰囲気とゆとりある主寝室
Master bedroom with a comfortable atmosphere and spaciousness

2
様々な使い方ができる洋室
Multi-purpose Western-style room

3
バスルーム
Bathroom

4
機能性とインテリア性を兼ね備えたキッチン
Functional kitchen also contributing to the interior design

5
洗面室：ウッドテイストが時にはあたたかく、時には爽やかに主張する
Washroom: A touch of wood gives a sense of warmth or freshness from time to time.

広尾 quarto
HIROO quarto
F.L.E.G. INTERNATIONAL CO., LTD.

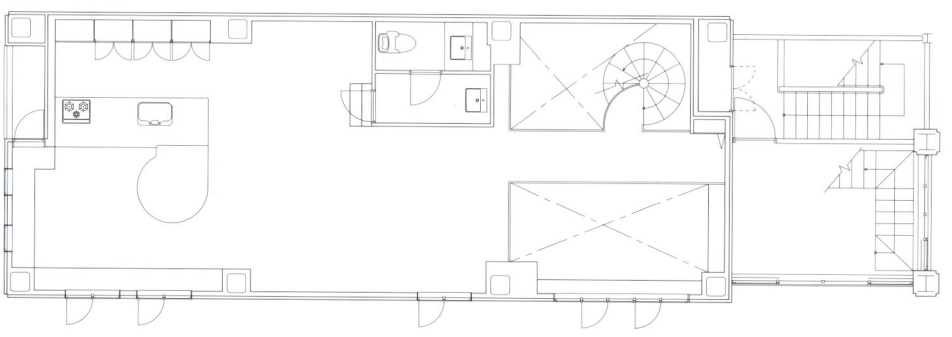

10F

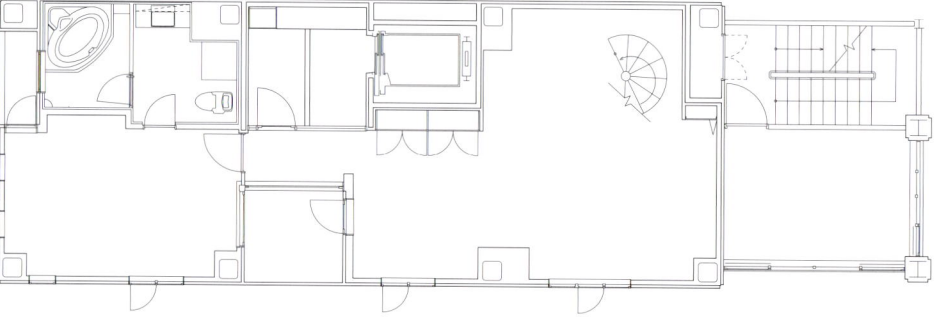

9F

Data	
Title	
	HIROO quarto
Developer	
	F.L.E.G. INTERNATIONAL CO., LTD.
Location	
	Shibuya-ku, Tokyo
Structure	
	S (RC in part)
Completion	
	September, 2005
Materials	
Public Floor :	tile
Interior Wall :	cloth
Interior Floor :	flooring

1
エントランス：ホールも白で統一されている
Entrance: The hall is also in white.

2
上階リビングルームからダイニング・キッチンを臨む
The dining room-cum-kitchen seen from the living room on the upper floor

3
下階リビングルーム
The living room on the lower floor

4
間接照明で演出されたダイニング・キッチン
The dining room-cum-kitchen illuminated by indirect lighting

1
上階リビングルームからブリッジを臨む
The bridge seen from the living room on the upper floor

2
ベットルーム
Bedroom

3
広々とした明るい雰囲気のバス・サニタリールーム
Spacious bathroom and the sanitary room giving a gay atmosphere

エグゼクティブやセレブの方に好まれる都心の高級邸宅地「広尾」「恵比寿」からの徒歩圏に位置している。明治通り沿いに白亜の城をイメージさせる秀麗で真っ白な外観。"贅のあるゆとり"を追求した住空間は、スタイルにこだわる都会派を想い描いたゆとりの広さと機能美を併せ持つメゾネットプラン。また、都市生活を守るセキュリティーはエレベーターから直接、自分のフロアにアクセスする安心のシステムを採用している。

The site is in a walking distance from such luxurious residential areas as Hiroo and Ebisu, highly preferred by executives and celebrities. The building along the Meiji Street has a graceful white facade inspiring a castle. The living space in pursuit of "comfort in luxury" is a combination of maisonette type offering spaciousness and functional beauty for urban residents who want to lead a stylish lifestyle. To ensure security in the city and provide a sense of safety provided is direct access to the unit from the elevator.

マリナゲートタワー
cotton harbor Marina Gate Tower

JFE Urban Development / Mitsubishi Estate Co., Ltd. / Nomura Real Estate Development Co., Ltd.
Hisato Tanabe (Mitsubishi Jisho Sekkei Inc.) / Mitsubishi Jisho Sekkei Inc.

コットンハーバー地区は、みなとみらい21地区につづき、新たな進化を始めた横浜港エリアのリーディングプロジェクト。そこは自然の恵みをたっぷり受ける、美しい海辺の街。住宅をはじめ、商業施設、ハーバーパーク（星野町公園）など多彩な施設ゾーンによって構成されている。コットンハーバー地区の住宅が求めてきたのは、建築だけではなく、その敷地も含めた環境と構成の美しさ。まるで美術館の庭を眺めているかのような風景と端正な住宅が響きあう、いわば、「MOMA＝ミュージアム・オブ・モダンアート」の美。「マリナゲートタワー」はこうした考え方のひとつの集大成。敷地を緑で包み込み、入口からつづく風景の連なりに建築が調和し、住む人が絵になるような豊かさがここに生まれる。求めたのは、刻一刻と変化する横浜港の表情に呼応する、上質で優雅なタワーデザイン。森の緑、空の青さ、太陽の光、そして生活する人々‥。そうした自然の色や人々の営みが織りなす色彩を活かすため、ファサードのデザインは「白」を基調に表現。ガラスパネルには風景が映し出され、光と陰影のリズムに美しく変化する。積層する白い壁面とほのかな曲線が、透明感と輝きに満ちた姿を描く。空や太陽の移ろいに合わせ、刻一刻と変化する外観の印象。ファサードのデザインテーマのひとつ「陰影のリズム＝Rhythm & Shadows」を実現するために、水平リブ（出っ張り）をバルコニーサイドの跳出しパネルの表面に設けている。白を基調とした外壁が、太陽の光によって美しく描かれる陰影を一層際立たせ、建物全体にリズミカルで豊かな表情を創り出す。

The development of the Cotton Harbor area is a leading project of Yokohama harbor area on a new stage of its evolution, following the Minatomirai 21 area project. This new town at a beautiful seaside fully enjoys the nature's blessings in various ways and is composed of zones with different characters including residential area, commercial facilities and a harbor park (Hoshino-cho Park). What is required for the design of houses in the Cotton Harbor area is not only the quality of architecture but also the beauty of surroundings and configuration including the individual sites. Elegant houses are in perfect harmony with the scenery, letting one feel as if one were looking at a museum garden. It is, as it were, a beautiful scene taken from "MOMA = Museum of Modern Art". The Marina Gate Tower is an epitome of the concept. On the site abundantly covered with green, the buildings perfectly match a series of scenes starting from the entrance, all creating richness in life where residents appear as if they were part of a painting. Totally sought is the fine quality and elegant design of the tower constantly responding to ever-changing Yokohama-harbor. To take advantage of colors given by nature and people leading everyday life in the area including green of the forest, blue of the sky and gold of the sunshine, the color of white is selected as the base of the facade design. The scenery reflected on the glass panels picturesquely changes with the rhythms of lights and shades. Accumulated layers of white walls and gentle curves draws a shape with a sense of transparency and brightness. Minute by minute, the exterior of the building gives a different impression with the changing colors of the sky and the sun. To realize one of the design themes of the facade, "Rhythm & Shades", horizontal ribs are installed on the surface of structural panels on balcony sides. The white-based exterior walls emphasizes the shadows beautifully drawn by the sunlight, creating different rhythms and expressions to the whole building.

Data

Title
 cotton harbor Marina Gate Tower

Developer
 JFE Urban Development
 Mitsubishi Estate Co., Ltd.
 Nomura Real Estate Development Co.,Ltd.

Design Produce
 Hisato Tanabe
 (Mitsubishi Jisho Sekkei Inc.)

Architect
 Mitsubishi Jisho Sekkei Inc.

Location
 Yokohama city, Kanagawa

Site area
 5,730.00m²

Building area
 1,688.30m²

Total floor area
 33,089.91m²

Structure
 RC (S in part)

Completion
 November, 2008

Materials
 Exterior Wall :
  sprayed coating, ceramic tile
 Public Wall :
  painting
 Public Floor :
  tile, flooring

	2	3
1	4	
	5	

1
端正な造形に込められた、エントランスの気品。ランドスケープの美しさやタワーの佇まいを象徴する水辺と木々、伸びやかなキャノピーが印象的。
The entrance gives a sense of elegance through its graceful design. Impressive are the pool, trees and extended canopies symbolizing the beauty of the landscape and the presence of the tower.

2
敷地配置図
Site Plan

3
伸びやかな窓辺を光と緑の庭が彩る二層吹き抜けのエントランスホール
Bright sunlight and green trees and plants are outside the windows of the entrance hall in the 2-story well.

4
モダンなインテリアで統一された「ガーデンラウンジ」。窓辺に広がる美しいテラスビューガーデンに呼応する
The Garden Lounge with a totally modern interior goes well with the beautiful Terrace View Garden.

5
ドラマティックな眺めと憩うスカイラウンジ。スタイリッシュな空間デザインのなかで、穏やかにやすらぎ、語らう、至福の時間
The Sky Lounge offers a dramatic view and blissful time for comfort and small talks in this stylish spatial design.

Marina Gate Tower | 111

E-1a type Chocolate Slow Days

海辺のどこかゆっくりとしたリズムに、シンクロする空間。日常の忙しさを忘れ、心が落ち着くやすらぎに浸るには、重厚で味があり、芳醇さを物語るジャトバテイストの木の温もりがよく似合う。御影石をあしらい、やや強めのコントラストを描いた玄関を入って奥へ。リビング・ダイニングでは、永い時間を自分とともに過ごしてきたお気に入りのモノたちが、ずっとそこにあったかのようにしっくりと馴染み、豊かな深みを生み出すような空間の包容力がある。味わいのある空間に、海辺のスローな時が流れる。

E-1a type: Chocolate Slow Days

The space keeps pace with a somehow slow rhythm at the seaside. To forget a busy everyday life and enjoy relaxing comfort, best suitable is warmth of wood with a texture of dignified, favorable and mellow Jatoba. Through the granite-floored entrance into the living-dining space, one finds one's long-time favorite goods perfectly fit the room as if they were always there. This rich, spacious room embraces everything, and in its elegance, time on the seaside slowly passes.

Data

Title
 Chocolate Slow Days E-1a type
Area
 82.61m^2
Materials
 Interior Wall :
  vinyl cloth
 Interior Floor :
  natural stone, flooring, carpet

A-2a type　Mint Sugar Bay
パノラマウィンドウに広がる空にシンクロするように、室内にもプレーンでピュアな、飾らない心地よさが続いていく。優しい色合いのなかにもエレガントな雰囲気を忘れない、マリナゲートタワーならではの上質さ。大理石で床をあしらい印象的な優美さを醸し出す玄関に、それが象徴されている。ふんわりと柔らかく包み込まれるような、どこかリゾートの薫りを感じさせる空気感。豪華に飾るのではなく、むしろ大切なものだけを残しシンプルに描くことで、人の姿や暮らしの彩りが引き立っていく。

A-2a type: Mint Sugar Bay
As if inspired by the blue sky outside the panoramic window, the interior design is simple, plain and pure. Gentle colors in an elegant atmosphere characterize the superiority of the Marina Gate Tower, symbolized by the marble-floored entrance that produces an impressive grace. The tower offers a feeling somehow suggesting a resort, embracing residents gently and softly. Instead of implementing luxurious interior decorations, the design keeps only important elements in a simple manner, highlighting the people and their lives in the tower.

1	4
2	5
3	6

1
リビング・ダイニング・書斎：伸びやかな広がりがある味わい深い空間
This living and dining room with a study is spacious with an elegant design.

2
リビングルームの付随した書斎スペース
The living room accompanies a space to be used as a study.

3
ダイニングと連動した開放的なキッチン
The dining-cum-kitchen gives a sense of spaciousness.

4
リビング・ダイニング：美しい淡灰白色の木材・センを使用したインテリアテイストが優しい雰囲気を醸し出す
Living-dining room: Beautiful ash gray wood of castor aralia is used to create a gentle atmosphere in the interior.

5
夜の照明に優しく浮かびあがるリビング・ダイニング
The living-dining room softly highlighted by the night illumination

6
明るく華やかな空気を創るオープンキッチン
The open kitchen creates a bright and gay atmosphere.

1	
2	

1
心地いい目醒めを誘う、やすらぎのベッドルーム
In this comfortable bedroom, even waking up is a cozy experience.

2
ビュー・パウダールーム：鏡を見上げれば、窓辺に開放的な景色が広がる
View powder room: When one looks up the mirror, one can also see an extensive view of the town outside the windows.

Data	
Title	
Mint Sugar Bay A-2a type	
Area	
87.92m²	
Materials	
Interior Wall :	
vinyl cloth	
Interior Floor :	
natural stone, flooring, carpet	

タワーレジデンストーキョー
Tower Residence Tokyo
ORIX Real Estate Corporation / IRIE MIYAKE ARCHITECTS & ENGINEERS

1
大きなシンボルツリーのあるエントランス外観
The exterior of the entrance with the big symbol tree.

2
敷地配置図：都心に向かって大きく開かれる扇フォルム。周辺環境との調和を考えながら、眺望、日照、プライバシーに配慮し、居住性の良さを追求している
Site layout: The exterior on the side of the fan-like footprint faces the city center. While attention is paid to the harmony and integrity with the surrounding environment, consideration is given to views, sunlighting and privacy to optimize the amenity.

Data

Title
Tower Residence Tokyo

Developer
ORIX Real Estate Corporation

Architect
IRIE MIYAKE ARCHITECTS & ENGINEERS

Location
Taito-ku, Tokyo

Site area
2,543.91m²

Building area
1,139.12m²

Total floor area
33,872.39m²

Structure
RC (S in part)

Completion
January, 2008

Materials
Exterior Wall :
  tile
Public Wall :
  brick, tile, glass curtain wall
Public Floor :
  marble, granite, tile

歴史を知ると、土地の価値がわかる。昔から発展している場所には人のエネルギーが集まっている。独特の地場として静かに醸成され、そこに住む人々の息吹が自然に溶け込んでいる。17世紀の江戸時代には、皇居のあった江戸城を中心として、商業エリアだった日本橋、そして賑わいのある浅草界隈に人と文化が集まっていた。まさにその真ん中に美しく柔らかに佇むタワーレジデンストーキョー。そのデザインは、タワーレジデンスにおける新しい方向性を示すものとして永く記憶されるかもしれない。都心に向けて開かれた扇形フォルムが意味するもの。様々な表情を見せる個性的なシンボル。ランドマークタワーとなるのはもちろん、周辺環境との調和を保ちながら、居住性の高さとここに住まう歓びを存分に感じることのできるデザイン性の高さ。ここから住まいの理想が見えてくる。

Learning the history means learning the value of the land. Every place with a long history of development is a gathering place of people and their energy. It has grown as a unique locality naturally integrated with the energy. Nihonbashi is one of the commercial areas surrounding the Edo Castle in the 17th century in the Edo Era, and the Asakusa area always with a good crowd is the focal point of people and culture. Beautifully and silently standing Tower Residence Tokyo is built in between these areas whose design may be remembered for a long time as a landmark to represent a new direction of tower residence designs. Its exterior on the side of the fan-like footprint facing toward the city center symbolizes its meaning in the context of the city, and unique features of the tower show changing faces over time. Its sophisticated design enables residents to enjoy excellent habitability and pleasure of living in it while making the building as a landmark tower well-balanced in the surrounding environments. The tower shows the ideal of residence.

| 1 |
| 2 |
| 3 |

1
明るく開放感のあるエントランスホール。天然大理石の階段など、上質な佇まいに包まれる空間に仕上がっている

This well-lit entrance hall with a sense of spaciousness is finished as a space to give a quality atmosphere, for example, by natural marble stairs.

2
重厚な雰囲気で本が読めるライブラリー
One can enjoy reading in the library with a sense of dignity.

3
屋上に設えた居住者専用のルーフトップガーデン。芝が敷き詰められ、ベンチを設置した眺望庭園

The rooftop garden on the top of the tower is exclusive for residents. It is a lawn-covered view garden with benches.

Tower Residence Tokyo

エッセンシャル・シック・モダン
Essential Chic Modern 130A type
FORWARD STYLE

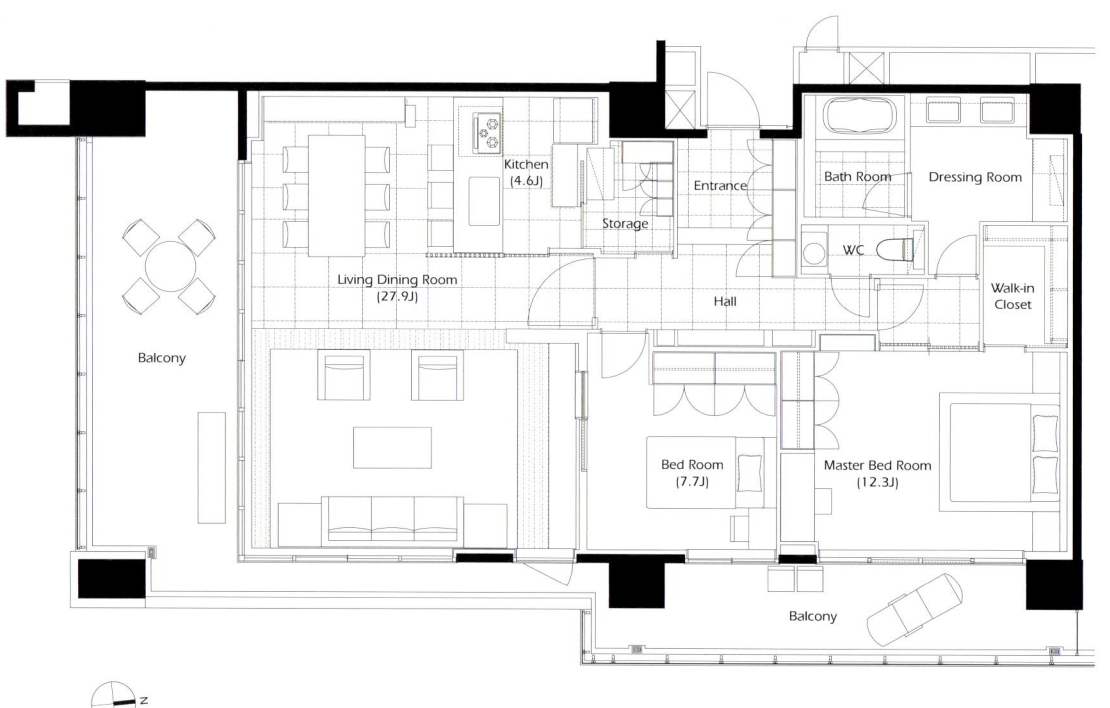

Data
Title
  Essential Chic Modern 130A type
Designer / Architect
  FORWARD STYLE
Area
  126.49m²
Materials
  Interior Wall :
    cloth, stone
  Interior Floor :
    artifical stone, flooring, carpet
Photo
  Nacása & Partners Inc.

	2	
1	3	4
	5	

1
リビング・ダイニングからバルコニーを臨む
The balcony seen from the living-dining area

2
リビングルームの石壁には丸窓を設けてあり、夜にはリビングの灯りがベッドルームに仄かに投影されるように光の演出を施している
The stonewall of the living room has a round window, and the light from the living area is softly projected into the bedroom, giving a special effect of light.

3
天然大理石が敷き詰められている、広々としたエントランス。天井までの全面収納を備え、風格のある表情で迎えてくれる
The entrance is covered with natural marble. The storage reaching up to the ceiling is provided to welcome residents in an elegant atmosphere.

4
ダークブラウンとのコントラストが美しいダイニング。間接照明を施した天井と光の柱を効果的に配置。壁際には上質なピックルドオークの棚を設えている
The dining area enhances its beauty in contrast with the color of dark brown. The ceiling indirectly lit and the light columns are effectively arranged. Pickled oak shelves are equipped by the wall.

5
ミニバーを備え、シックな色調で統一された、落ち着きのある主寝室。和のテイストを活かし、垂直方向の建具と水平方向の家具とを絶妙なバランスでコーディネート
The master bedroom designed with chic colors and with a mini-bar gives a sense of relaxation. Taking advantage of the Japanese taste, delicately balanced is a combination of the vertical fittings and horizontally arranged furniture.

Tower Residence Tokyo

1
2
3

1
幅約2.9mの広々としたバルコニー。都心の素晴らしい眺望とともにここだけの特別な癒しの空間を創造する

The spacious balcony as wide as about 2.9 meters offers a wonderful view of the city center, creating a unique and special space for healing.

2
ゆったりとしたパウダールームには、ワイドミラー、ダブルボウルを設置している

The expansive powder room is equipped with a wide mirror and double sinks.

3
壁には天然大理石を、床や浴槽まわりには天然御影石を使用した、高級感溢れるバスルーム。テレビも楽しめ、快適なバスタイムが過ごせる

The bathroom gives a sense of quality, thanks to employment of natural marble for the wall and natural granite for the floor and bathtub. One can enjoy a relaxed, comfortable bathtime, watching TV.

天然大理石の広々としたエントランスからリビングルームに入ると、天井高3mの圧倒的な広がりを感じる。満ちているのは高級リゾートで体感する開放感。プライベートゾーンとパブリックゾーンを柔らかく分離。本物の天然素材を厳選して惜しみなく使用し、シックなダークブラウンで統一された印象的な空間。

When one enters the living room through a spacious entrance area with natural marble, one will be impressed with an overwhelming expansion of the room with a ceiling height of 3 meters. The room is filled with a sense of spaciousness that one enjoys in deluxe resort. The private and public zones of the unit are subtly separated. Genuine natural materials are carefully selected and unsparingly used in this impressive space consistently designed in the color of chic dark brown.

スタイリッシュ・ピュア・ナチュラル
Stylish Pure Natural 80C type
FORWARD STYLE

1

扇フォルムによって生まれた約20.6畳の広々としたリビング・ダイニング

The living-dining area as wide as 30 square meters is created, thanks to the fan-like footprint of the unit.

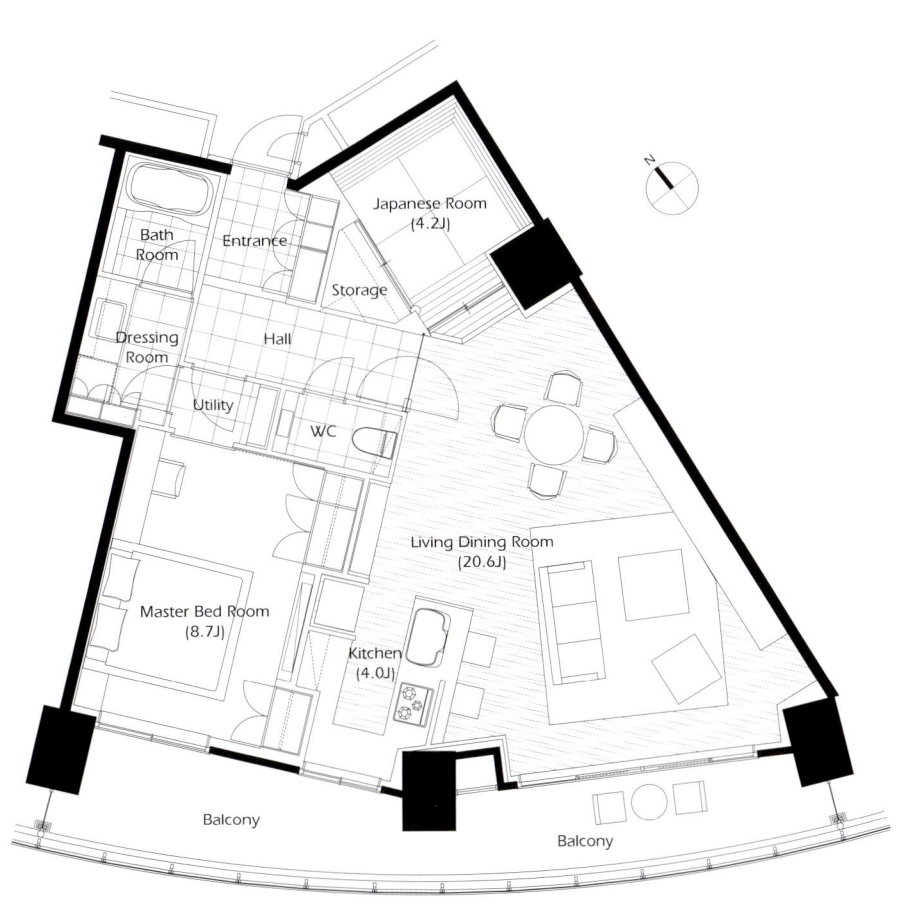

Data

Title
　Stylish Pure Natural 80C type

Designer / Architect
　FORWARD STYLE

Area
　83.37m²

Materials
　Interior Wall :
　　cloth
　Interior Floor :
　　tile, flooring, carpet

Photo
　Nacása & Partners Inc.

Tower Residence Tokyo

扇フォルムがもたらす、透明な開放感。約20.6畳の広々としたリビングルームの開放感と約11.6mのワイドスパンは、扇フォルムならではのもの。明るく統一された色調とともに、透明感あるスタイリッシュな空間が伸びやかに広がる。窓に面したキッチン、琉球風畳や和紙を使ってモダンに設えられた和室など、細部に至るまでこだわりを備えている。

The fan-like footprint of the unit uniquely gives a sense of unconfining spaciousness in the living room with an area of around 30 square meters and a wide span of about 11.6 meters. A stylish space with a sense of transparency comfortably expands in consistently light colors. Careful attention is paid to every details of the design including the kitchen facing the window and the Japanese-style room with a sense of modernity by using the Ryukyu-like tatami mats and Japanese paper.

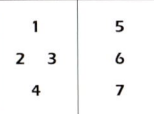

1

リビング・ダイニング：都心の眺望とともに、ホワイト基調の上質な明るさに満ち溢れている開放的な空間

The living-dining area is spacious and luminous thanks to its view of the city and white-based design.

2

エントランスとリビングルームをつなぐ、スタイリッシュな廊下。ホワイトオークの色調と相まって、明るく洗練された空気感を醸し出す

The stylish corridor connecting the entrance and the living room. Its white oak texture creates a light and sophisticated atmosphere.

3

窓に面している開放的なコの字形のセミオープンキッチン

The U-shaped semi-open kitchen faces the window, giving a spacious impression.

4

琉球風畳のモダンな和室。格子越しに漏れる光の表情、和紙を使ったこだわりの設えで、ゲストルームとしてはもちろん、生け花や茶道などにも使える空間

The modern, Japanese-style room has Ryukyu-style tatami mats and can be used not only as a guestroom but also a tea or flower arrangement room, thanks to light through grating and ample use of Japanese paper.

5

ホワイトオーク特有のナチュラルな雰囲気に包まれる主寝室。壁一面の収納棚、女性のためのドレッサースペースなど、使い勝手を考えた設えを整えている

The master bedroom gives a natural atmosphere unique to its white oak material. One of the walls is efficiently dedicated for storage while a dresser space is provided for ladies. The room is finished with due consideration of convenience.

6

バスルーム：大型のバスタブに加えて、ワイドミラー、ドレッサーカウンター、スライドバー、収納棚などを備え、機能性と快適性を高めている

The bathroom has not only a large bathtub but also a wide mirror, a dresser counter, slide bars and a storage shelf for functionality and comfort.

7

質感に溢れたパウダールーム。細部のデザインにまでこだわった上質な洗面カウンター

The powder room with a superb sense of texture is equipped with a carefully designed, quality counter.

Stylish Pure Natural 70B type

2つの居室の連続性を活かして、あたかもひとつのオープンな空間のように感じられるように大胆な発想でコーディネート。天井高約2.75mの広がりを生かしたナチュラルな空間として仕上がっている。上品なテクスチャーの質感とともに、淡いカラーリングで全体を統一。朝の陽光を享受できる、開放的な居住スペースが広がっている。

Stylish Pure Natural 70B type

Taking advantage of the continuity of two living rooms, the unit is designed with the bald idea of making them as a single open space but appears as a natural expansion, thanks to its roomy ceiling height of 2.75 meters. The interior is totally coordinated with light coloring with a sense of volume based on its elegant texture. It is an open residential space to enjoy early morning sunshine.

1
2
3

1

リビング・ダイニング：ホワイトオークとウォールナットならではのナチュラルな空気感に満ちている。透かしのある欄間を設けることで、陽光溢れる空間となっている

The living-dining area based on white oak and walnut gives a natural atmosphere. Transoms let sunlight come into the room.

2

寝室とリビング・ダイニングを臨む。DENを配することで居室のつながりを活かしたオープンな空間を演出し、プライベート性にも配慮。明るいリビングに対して、寝室はアイボリーとダークブラウンの色調で穏やかなやすらぎ感を大切にしている

The bedroom and the living dining area. Providing the unit with a den gives the space with a sense of openness, continuity and privacy. In contrast with a light colored living space, the bedroom emphasizes comfortable sense of relaxation thanks to its ivory and dark brown coloring.

3

DENからベッドルームを臨む。横格子を配し、一体感を持たせながらDENと寝室を柔らかくセパレート。しかもグレーペンミラーを設けて開放感を演出

The bedroom seen from the den: The den and the bedroom are subtly separated while keeping a sense of continuity, added with an open impression by employing gray smoke color glass.

LAZONA
Kawasaki
Residence

ラゾーナ川崎レジデンス
LAZONA Kawasaki Residence
TOSHIBA BUILDING Co., Ltd. / Mitsui Fudosan Co., Ltd. / KAJIMA Corporation

Data
Title
LAZONA Kawasaki Residence
Developer
TOSHIBA BUILDING Co., Ltd.
Mitsui Fudosan Co., Ltd.
Architect
KAJIMA Corporation
Location
Kawasaki city, Kanagawa
Site area
16,092.25m²
Building area
7,131.95m²
Total floor area
77,495.34m²
Structure
RC
Completion
March, 2007
Materials
Exterior Wall :
ceramic tile, sprayed coating
natural stone
Public Wall :
ceramic tile
Public Floor :
natural stone, flooring, carpet

東京山の手の上質な文化とエキゾシズム溢れる横浜のエキスが触発しあい、新たなカルチャーシーンを生み出す川崎。首都圏有数のターミナル駅前に残されたこの川崎西口の広大な敷地に、「大きな屋根に覆われた街」というコンセプトをもとにした、JR川崎駅と直結した大型商業施設。さらに、総戸数667戸の大型集合住宅がつくり出すこの新しい街こそ、進・川崎を完成させる大きな柱となるだろう。「人と人の関係を再生」させ、「人と自然のあり方を再生」させ、「自然な自分に再生」させてくれる街。この３つの「再生」によるつながりがあるからこそ、人と人の出会いが輝く街となり、プラスニュースな街だといえる。高い交通・生活利便と、駅前なのに郊外を思わせる安らぎと潤いを両立させ、溢れる緑の中でくつろげる、この「街」。川崎の中心になっていくのだろう、この「街」。この街は、やはり、LAZO＝つながり、ZONA＝エリアという２つの言葉を組み合わせることでさらなる広がりを持つ名前にふさわしい。

Kawasaki is a town where sophisticated culture of Yamanote area in Tokyo and exotic essence of Yokohama meet to create a new cultural scene in between. In the vast site on the west side of Kawasaki, one of the biggest terminal stations in the Metropolitan Area, large-scale commercial facilities directly connected to the station, having a concept of "the town under a large roof" and a 667-unit high-rise condominium are built to add the final piece to complete the new shape of Kawasaki to come. It is a place to "revive interpersonal relations," "redefine the human-nature relation," and "refresh one to bring oneself back." These three processes of "renewal" are links to highlight human encounters and to invent something new. Excellent convenience in life and transportation is integrated with comfort and richness reminding one of suburbs in spite of its station-front location, and one can relax oneself in the environment rich in green. This area will become the core of Kawasaki and is suitable for its inspiring name created from a combination of "LAZO" (connection) and "ZONA" (area).

1	2
	3
	4

1

エントランスアプローチ：桜並木に沿ったルーバー状の美しいデザイン・ウォールがモダンな印象を与える

Entrance approach: The beautifully designed louver-like walls along the rows of cherry trees give a modern impression.

2

セントラルタワーとレフトウイングをつなぐように足元に水盤が配されている。敷地全体を緑の樹木が包み込み、都会の喧噪を忘れる安らぎと潤いに溢れた外構計画

A pool is set up along the walls connecting the Central Tower and the Left Wing. In the exterior planning, the site is surrounded by green trees, enabling one to forget the hustles and bustles of the city with its comfortable and relaxing atmosphere.

3

エントランス：列柱が並び、両サイドに水と緑が配されたゆとりある空間。

Entrance: This spacious space accommodates rows of columns with pools and plants on both sides of the passageway.

4

エントランスホールの中ほど、広々とした芝生のプライベートガーデンに面したアクアラウンジ。らせん階段のある２層のスペース

The Aqua Lounge in the middle of the entrance hall faces expansive lawns of the private garden. This 2-story space has spiral stairs.

LAZONA Kawasaki Residence | 127

アーバン
URBAN

進・川崎の住まいにふさわしく、シックで洗練された都会的な空間を、シャープでスタイリッシュなさまざまなディテールが生活をモダンに演出してくれる。

Suitable for a residence in new Kawasaki in progress, various strong and stylish design details contribute to modern impression of this chic and sophisticated urban space.

Standard Plan

写真はモデルルーム。標準プランとは異なります。
Photos are the model room. They are different from the standard plan somewhat.

Data

Title
  URBAN

Area
  95.73m²

Materials
  Interior Wall :
    cloth
  Interior Floor :
    natural stone, flooring, carpet

	2	3
1	4	

1
コーナーサッシュが開放感を創り出す、スタイリッシュなリビングルーム
Sashes at the corner give a sense of openness in this stylish living room.

2
高級レストランの一角を思わせるような都会的でお洒落なモノトーンのダイニングルーム
This urban, sophisticated, monotone-based dining room reminds one of a high-class restaurant.

3
白のカウンターに黒の壁面や扉がシャープな感じを演出しながら、カウンター下の壁面はモノトーンのモザイクタイルが、イタリアンテイストを思わせるモダンなキッチン
While the contrast between the white counter and black walls and doors gives a well-defined impression, the walls below the counter is mosaique-tiled to suggest an Italian taste in this modern kitchen.

4
しっとりと落ち着いた上質なマスターベッドルーム
The master bedroom is gentle, comfortable and refined.

プレミアムホワイト
Premium White

Standard Plan
写真はモデルルーム。標準プランとは異なります。
Photos are the model room. They are different from the standard plan somewhat.

感度の高いミニマルな空間は、広がりとプライベート感を同時に創出。スタイリッシュなライフスタイルを提案してくれる。リビング、キッチン、ベッドルーム、そして水場までもが一体になった透明感あふれる空間。

This simple and sensitive space simultaneously creates a sense of expansion and that of privacy, proposing a stylish and sophisticated lifestyle. In this space with a transparent impression, totally integrated are the living room, kitchen, bedroom and even bathroom.

Data	
Title	Premium White
Area	61.03m²
Materials	Interior Wall : cloth
	Interior Floor : natural stone

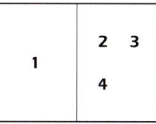

1
高感度な暮らしをさらにエネルギッシュにスタイリッシュにしてくれるリビングルーム
The living room further contributes to stylish, energetic and interest-sensitive life in this town.

2
エントランスホール：リビングへと続く廊下でさえも洗練された空間に仕上がっている
Entrance hall: Even the corridor leading to the living room is finished as a sophisticated space.

3
キッチンカウンターがそのままダイニングテーブルとなったスマートなキッチン
In this stylish kitchen, the kitchen counter also serves as the dining table "as-is".

4
ベッドルームから、ドレッシングルーム越しにバスルームを臨む
The bathroom seen from the bedroom beyond the dressing room.

1
2
3

1
ベッドルーム：間接照明で演出されたプレミアムな空間
Bedroom: This premium space is indirectly illuminated for a special atmosphere.

2
ゴージャスにしてクリーン。一日の始まりと終わりに、めり張りをつけてくれる高いデザイン性を持ったドレッシングルーム
This dressing room is gorgeous and clean with a sophisticated design to vary the pace of one's life at the beginning and end of the day.

3
リゾートホテルを思わせる優雅なバス
The graceful bathroom reminds one of a resort hotel.

パークシティ豊洲
Urban Dock Park City Toyosu

Ishikawajima-Harima Heavy Industries Co., Ltd. / Mitsui Fudosan Co., Ltd. / Michel J. Bedner (HBA)
Joint Venture of Sumitomo Mitsui Construction Co.,Ltd. And KAJIMA Corporation / Jun Mitsui (JMA)
Gen Kumagai · Eiki Danzuka (Eaethscape) / Hiroyasu Shouji / Atsushi Kaneda

Data

Title
Urban Dock Park City Toyosu

Developer
Ishikawajima-Harima Heavy Industries Co., Ltd.
Mitsui Fudosan Co., Ltd.

Design Consultant
Michel J. Bedner (HBA)

Architect
Joint Venture of Sumitomo Mitsui Construction Co.,Ltd.
And KAJIMA Corporation

Facade design
Jun Mitsui (JMA)

Landscape design
Gen Kumagai (Eaethscape)
Eiki Danzuka (Eaethscape)

Landscape lighting design
Hiroyasu Shouji (LIGHTDESIGN INC.)

Interior lighting design
Atsushi Kaneda
 (Worktecht Corporation)

Location
Koto-ku, Tokyo

Site area
28,900.05m²

Building area
Tower A : 7,612.01m²
Tower B : 5,657.45m²
Court C : 1,447.05m²

Total floor area
Tower A : 121,938.78m²
Tower B : 63,641.00m²
Court C : 5,580.28m²

Structure
Tower A : RC (S in part)
Tower B : RC (S+SRC in part)
Court C : RC

Completion
Tower B : January, 2008
Tower A, Court C : March, 2008

Materials
Exterior Wall :
 45x90tile, tile
Public Wall :
 natural stone, cloth
Public Floor :
 natural stone, flooring

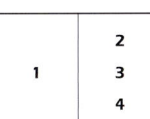

1
エントランスコート：アネックスの煌めく灯りや路面に埋め込まれた LED が放つプログラミングされた様々なパターン。美しい光に彩られた幻想的な光景
Entrance court: A fantastic scene is presented by bright lights from the annex, various preprogrammed patterns of LED's embedded in the passageway and other beautiful light sources.

2
海上公園：全長 800m もの海辺のプロムナード
Marine park: This seaside promenade stretches as long as 800 meters.

3
樹木に包まれ、光が迎えるセンタープロムナードは、エントランスと海へのアプローチとなっている
The center promenade surrounded by the trees and welcoming lights is the passage between the entrance and the sea.

4
敷地配置図
Site plan

Urban Dock Park City Toyosu | 135

1	4
2	5
3	6

1
Tower-A ロビー：世界に名だたるホテルのインテリアデザインを手がけるHBAと植物を素材とした造形で世界的に著名なダニエル・オスト氏のコラボレーション
Tower-A lobby: The design is the result of collaboration between HBA engaged in interior design of famous hotels in the world and Daniel Ost celebrated for his plant-based works.

2
エレベーターホール
Elevator hall

3
Tower-B ラウンジ：洗練された都会的なイメージで満たされたホテルライクな空間
Tower-B lounge: This hotel-like space gives a sophisticated, urban impression.

4
Tower-A スカイラウンジ：都市の雄大な景色を一望できる、バルコニー付のスカイラウンジ
Tower-A sky lounge: With a balcony, the sky lounge offers a great command of view of the city.

5
パノラマウィンドウが印象的なスカイラウンジに付随したTower-Bスカイデッキ。視界を遮るものがない東京湾のパノラマビュー
The sky deck of the Tower-B is adjacent to the sky lounge with an impressive panoramic window, offering a panoramic view of the Tokyo Bay with no obstruction.

6
ANNEXプール&ジェットバス：海に面した全面ガラス貼りの空間
ANNEX pool and jet bath: The glass-walled space faces the sea.

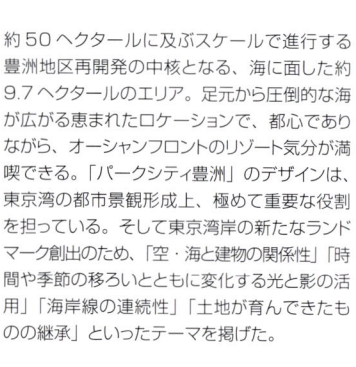

約50ヘクタールに及ぶスケールで進行する豊洲地区再開発の中核となる、海に面した約9.7ヘクタールのエリア。足元から圧倒的な海が広がる恵まれたロケーションで、都心でありながら、オーシャンフロントのリゾート気分が満喫できる。「パークシティ豊洲」のデザインは、東京湾の都市景観形成上、極めて重要な役割を担っている。そして東京湾岸の新たなランドマーク創出のため、「空・海と建物の関係性」「時間や季節の移ろいとともに変化する光と影の活用」「海岸線の連続性」「土地が育んできたものの継承」といったテーマを掲げた。

それぞれのプロフェッショナルが自由な発想のデザインで個性を発揮しつつ、調和のとれた海辺の美しい街並みの実現を目指してコラボレーションしている。シカゴ、バンクーバー、シドニーなど世界各地の国際都市は、水辺の環境を活かしながら発展してきた。街の発展は「水の力」を抜きにして語れない。東京で初めて暮らしに海を取り入れた「パークシティ豊洲」も、大いなる発展が期待できる。外観では大海原を悠々と航行する帆船がデザインイメージとなっている。輝く白を基調として、白を際立たせる淡いグリーンやサーモンカラーなどのナチュラルカラーも用いている。遠くから見ると白いタワー、近くにつれて他の色が見え、建物の表情が変わる。風をはらんだ帆のように穏やかな曲面を描く建物は太陽の光を受けて美しく輝く。デザインでは、形状の異なる3棟の個性を活かしながら、全体的にはひとつの街に見えるということを重視している。生花の「真（しん）・副（そえ）・体（たい）」のように、それぞれが役割を持ち、調和のある街を築いてゆく。

To serve as the core of the redevelopment project of the Toyosu area as wide as about 50 hectares, the condominium is located on the site of about 9.7 hectares facing the sea. It is a favorable location looking down the grand view of the sea, offering a sense of being in an ocean front resort while one is still in the megalopolis. The design of Park City Toyosu assumes an extremely important role in forming the urban landscape of the Tokyo Bay. In order to create a new landmark in the Tokyo Bay area, introduced are such themes as "relationship between the sky, the sea and the building," "utilization of light and shade that change with the passage of time and seasons," "continuity of the coastline," and "succession of what has been cultivated in the area." Individual professionals collaborate with each other to realize a beautiful landscape on the seaside while demonstrating their abilities in exploiting freely conceived designs. Chicago, Vancouver, Sydney and many other international cities in the world have been developed by taking advantage of their waterfront environments. No city can develop without the "power of water." So we can expect much development of Park City Toyosu, the first condominium in Tokyo to integrate the sea into its residents' lives. The design of its appearance inspires a sailboat slowly on a voyage in the ocean. Based on the color of shining white, the building also employs such natural colors as light green and salmon red to highlight the white. From a distance, it looks like a white tower, but when one comes near it, the building changes its expression. The architecture with gentle curves as if it were a sail in the wind beautifully shines in the sunlight. Its architectural design emphasizes that while three different shaped buildings have their own uniqueness and characteristics, they should give an integrated impression as a town. As if they were the three main branches in flower arrangements (the shin (truth) branch, the soe (supporting) branch and the hikae (moderating) branch,) each building has its own role to build a town in harmony.

JMAグレードアップ
JMA Grade-up

JMA / Jun Mitsui

Data

Title
  JMA Grade-up

Designer / Architect
  JMA / Jun Mitsui

Area
  100.12m²

Materials
  Interior Wall :
   cloth
  Interior Floor :
   marble, flooring

1	3
	4
2	5

1
開放感のあるリビング・ダイニング
Expansive living-dining room

2
白でコーディネートされた、大人の感性に美しく共鳴するエントランス。ニッチとアクセントウォールが透明感のある奥行きをもたらす
Coordinated in white, the entrance matches the taste of adults. Niches and accent walls give a sense of expansion and transparency.

3
リビングに付随したDEN。ライフスタイルに合わせ、色々な使い方が出来る
The den next to the living room can be used for different purposes to fit one's lifestyle.

4
透過性のあるバルコニー手摺りを採用し、外と室内の連続性を重視したリビング・ダイニング
Semi-transparent handrails are used for the balcony to maintain a sense of continuity between the outside and the inside of the living-dining room.

5
約2mの奥行きがあり、広々としたバルコニー
This wide balcony has a depth of about 2 meters.

Urban Dock Park City Toyosu

HBAプライムシティエスケープ
HBA Prime City Escape
HBA / Michel J. Bedner

1	2 3
	4

1
リビングからダイニング・キッチンを臨む
The dining kitchen seen from the living space

2
エントランスからマスターベッドルームを臨む
The master bedroom seen from the entrance

3
エントランス：クリスタルダウンライトを使用したラグジュアリーを極めた華やかな空間
Entrance hall: This gay and luxurious space uses crystal downlights.

4
ダイニングからバーカウンター付きのリビングを臨む。シックな落ち着きを感じるラグジュアリーな空間
The living space with the bar counter seen from the dining space. This space of luxury offers a sense of chic elegance.

Data

Title
HBA Prime City Escape

Designer / Architect
HBA / Michel J. Bedner

Area
180.39m²

Materials
Interior Wall :
 cloth
Interior Floor :
 granite, marble, flooring

Photo
Nacása & Partners Inc.

1
2
3

1

機能性と清潔感のある美しいキッチン
The beautiful yet functional and clean kitchen

2

マスターベッドルーム：大型の三面鏡がついた
ウォークインクロゼット
Master bedroom: The walk-in closet has three large mirrors.

3

落ち着いた雰囲気と、ゆとりある広さのマスター
ベッドルーム
The master bedroom offers a comfortable atmosphere and a roomy expansion space.

Brillia Grande Minatomirai OCEAN & PARK

Brilia Grande みなとみらい OCEAN & PARK
Brillia Grande Minatomirai OCEAN & PARK

Tokyo Tatemono Co., Ltd. / STARTS CORPORATION / COOP JC Tokyo Jyutaku Kyokyu Center
Nihon Sekkei, Inc.

穏やかな海の碧と、豊かな緑が織りなす絵のようなランドスケープ。まるで空に光を投げかけたような、太陽を映す高層ビルのスカイライン。みなとみらい。そこは世界に誇る国際都市・横浜の美しい港を舞台に咲く永遠のサンクチュアリ。地上30階建てのツインタワー「Brillia Grade みなとみらい」では2棟の建物をそのまま並べるのではなく、45°傾けたレイアウトを採用している。この変化に富んだ住宅配置は、ランドマークとしての美しさを際立たせるだけでなく、超高層でありながらも互いのボリュームで眺望や日照を遮ったり、住戸間で見合うこともないよう配慮された機能的な建築スタイル。建物の外観においても、独自の洗練された世界観を追求している。地上30階建てのファサードをシンボリックに演出するのは、白を基調にしたシンプルで爽快な外壁と、シルバーグレーのフレームデザイン、空の青さを映すガラスのバルコニーが織りなす透明感あふれるフォルム。周囲に広がる海や空の青さ、緑の風景をさわやかに受けとめる、伸びやかな佇まい。また全体的なプロポーションとしては、フラットな壁面と装飾を排したデザインにより、スタイリッシュな表情に仕上げている。いつの時代も輝きを失わない、普遍的な洗練を追求している。

A picturesque landscape seems to be painted in the gentle blue of the sea and the rich green of the trees. The skyline of high-rise buildings reflecting the sunshine appears as if they were rays of lights coming up into the sky. Minatomirai is an eternal sanctuary built in the beautiful port of Yokohama, world-renowned international city. 30-story twin towers of Brillia Grade Minatomirai are set at 45-degree angles, instead of being aligned in line. This arrangement not only emphasizes its beauty as a landmark but also offers functionality because, in spite of the towers' high-rise design, they don't obstruct any view or light and offer no direct line of sight into the units. The exterior of the architecture is also a result of pursuit of unique, sophisticated Weltanschauung. The facade of the 30-story buildings are symbolically produced by simple and clean, white-based outer walls, silver gray frames and glass balcony reflecting the blue of the sky. The well-defined appearance of the building perfectly fits with the blue of the surrounding sea and sky and the green of the landscape. The design eliminating flat walls and decorations gives a stylish expression and pursues a universal sense of sophistication that will never be aged.

Data

Title
Brillia Grande Minatomirai OCEAN & PARK

Developer
Tokyo Tatemono Co., Ltd.
STARTS CORPORATION
COOP JC Tokyo Jyutaku Kyokyu Center

Architect
Nihon Sekkei, Inc.

Location
Yokohama city, Kanagawa

Site area
8,117.79m²

Building area
5,519.45m²

Total floor area
73,342.78m²

Structure
RC (S in part)

Completion
November, 2007

Materials
Exterior Wall :
45x90 ceramic tile, sprayed coating
Public Wall :
marble, igneous rocks, EP
Public Floor :
granite, tile carpet

	2	3
1	4	
	5	

1
均整のとれたプロポーションと、ガラスなどの透明感あふれる素材を多用して、超高層でありながらも周囲に圧迫感を与えることのない美しいフォルム
Having a well-balance proportion and amply using glass and other transparent materials, the beautiful forms of the high-rise buildings don't give a sense of oppression in the landscape.

2
歩行者専用遊歩道から外観を臨む
The exterior seen from the pedestrian promenade

3
吹き抜けの空間に濃密な上質感が漂うエントランスホール
Entrance hall in the well gives a strong sense of quality.

4
街並みに洗練の風景を描き出すガラス貼りのエントランスファサード。シンプル&ミニマムをテーマにガラスウォールにルーバー状フィンが反復するデザインを施し、装飾を可能な限り排した大人のモダニズムを構築している
The entrance facade produces a sophisticated impression on the townscape. Based on the theme of "simple & minimal" design, it is applied with louver fins with the minimum decoration, representing mature modernism.

5
コンシェルジュが優しくおもてなしするロビー&フロント
The concierge offers a warm welcome in the lobby and at the front desk.

プレミアム・スタイル [90CO]
Premium Style [90CO]
Hitomi Beppu

「みなとみらい」の空と、美しく豊かな空間を独り占めしたい、という思いを叶えてくれるレジデンシャルなプラン。90㎡を超える贅沢な室内設計と、洗練された空間デザインによって、まさに邸宅と呼ぶにふさわしいクオリティを実現している。20畳を超えるリビングや、優雅で広々としたビューバスやパウダールーム、まるでショールームのようなアイランドキッチンなど、すべてにゴージャスな空間を追求。インテリアもそれにふさわしく、シックで知的なダーク系の素材を用い、大人の寛ぎの空間を描いている。

This residential plan makes your dream of possessing the sky of "Minatomirai" as well as beautiful and rich spaces. The luxurious interior and sophisticated spatial designs gives an area of more than 90 square meters with a quality comparable to a "mansion." Its 30-square-meter living room, elegant and expansive view bath and powder rooms, an island kitchen all produce a gorgeous atmosphere, matched with the interior design using chic and intelligent, dark-colored materials suitable for a relaxing space for adults.

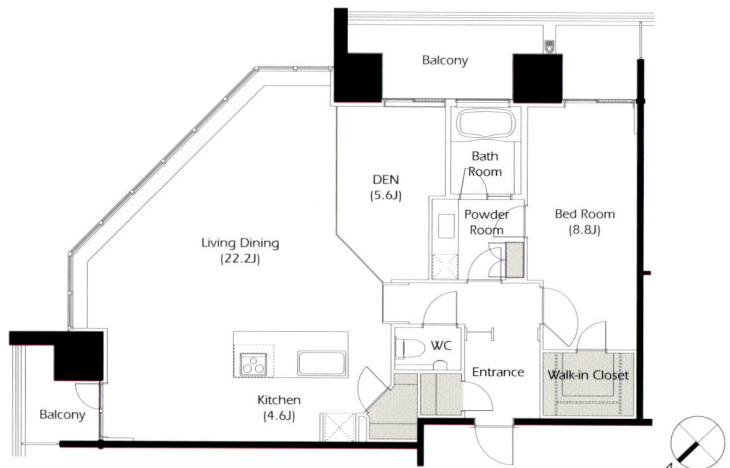

Data

Title
Premium Style [90CO]

Designer
Hitomi Beppu

Area
91.08㎡

Materials
Interior Wall:
vinyl cloth
Interior Floor:
marble, flooring

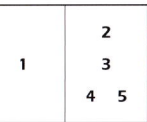

1
リビング・ダイニング：木の味わい深い質感と降り注ぐ陽光で演出されている
The living-dining space: Wood-based design imparts richness to the sun-drenched room.

2
まるで「みなとみらい」と溶け合うようなワイドなパノラマウィンドウが広がる贅沢な眺めのリビング・ダイニング
The living-dining area has a wide, panoramic window system with a grand view, giving an impression as if the space is part of "Minatomirai."

3
ゆったりとした主寝室
Roomy master bedroom

4
海辺の風景に心と身体のリラックスを委ねる広々としたビューバス
Spacious bath with a view of the port and the sea for physical and mental relaxation

5
リビングとの段差によって創り上げた優雅なDENスペース
This elegant den space takes advantage of a step with the living room.

スーペリアル・スタイル [80AO] [60DP]
Superior Style [80AO] / [60DP]
Yuri Sadogawa

Superior Style [80AO]

「みなとみらい」の豊かな眺望を住まいの一部に感じられるような、バルコニー面に3室をレイアウトしたワイドスパン設計のプラン。80㎡のゆとりある空間の中でリビングを中心に配置し、家族の理想的なコミュニケーションを育めるよう考えられている。窓辺の景色を採り込んだリビング&キッチン、ゆとりある主寝室、各所に設置した豊かな収納スペースが、想像以上に伸びやかな暮らしを実現。また、インテリアテイストでは、自然を感じさせる、落ち着いたブラウン系でまとめ、モダンでナチュラルな生活シーンを創造している。

Superior Style [80AO]

This plan offers a wide span floor where three rooms are facing the balcony to integrate a rich view of "Minatomirai" into part of the unit. Centered on the living space, this 80-square-meter unit is designed for promoting ideal communication among family members. A sense of expansion that is more than one expects from the layout is thanks to the living room and kitchen with an excellent command of view, the roomy main bedroom and ample storage spaces provided as appropriate. The interior is based on comfortable brown that reminds one of nature to produce a scene for a modern and natural lifestyle.

Superior Style [60DP]

「みなとみらい」の都会的で洗練された街の空気感を意識して創り上げた、シンプルでスタイリッシュな暮らしを自由に満喫できる機能的でスマートなプラン。ワイドサッシを採用したリビングを中心に、ホワイエの扉をフレキシブルに使い分けられる間仕切り型にしたり、廊下面積を抑えることで、実際以上に広がりがある空間を実現。また、インテリアテイストにおいても、白を基調にした、空に溶け込むような透明感あふれる空間を創造。生成やコットンの手触りのような温もりが、住まいを優しく包み込む。

Superior Style [60DP]

This sophisticated functional plan is designed to match the chic, urban atmosphere of "Minatomirai" to enable its residents to freely and flexibly lead a simple and stylish life. A space that appears more expansive than its actual area focused around the living room with wide sashes is realized by employing a flexible partition-type door for the foyer and reducing the area of corridors. The white-based interior produces a space with a sense of transparency and integration with the sky. The residence offers warmth reminding one of unbleached or cotton cloth.

Data

Title	Title
Superior Style [80AO]	Superior Style [60DP]
Designer	**Designer**
Yuri Sadogawa	Yuri Sadogawa
Area	**Area**
80.66㎡	64.15㎡
Materials	**Materials**
Interior Wall : vinyl cloth	Interior Wall : vinyl cloth
Interior Floor : marble, flooring	Interior Floor : marble, flooring

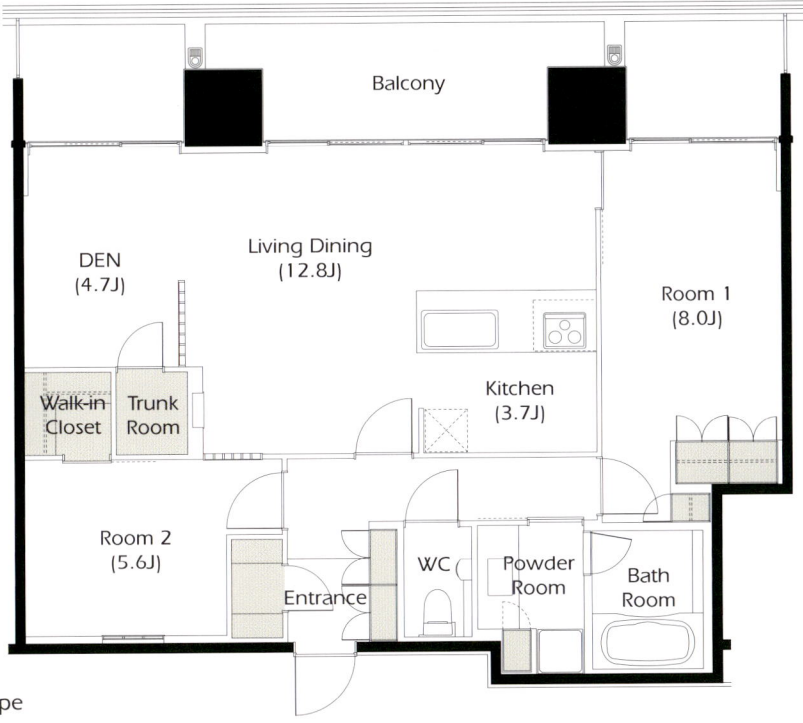

80AO type

| | 2 | 3 |
|1| 4 | |

1
ワイドスパン設計によって開口部を大きく広げた明るく爽やかなリビング・ダイニング・キッチン

The wide-span floor design provides the living room with a combined dining room and kitchen with a big opening, giving a well-lit, comfortable impression.

2
味わい深いダークブラウンのフローリングと白いクロスが印象的なリビング・ダイニング

The living room with a combined dining room and kitchen features sophisticated dark brown flooring and white cloth.

3
優雅な折上天井とハイサッシュを採用した明るく開放的な主寝室

The master bedroom has a bright and open impression with its elegant coved ceiling and a high sash.

4
ホームシアターにも最適な空間DEN

The den is suitable for a home theater system.

Brillia Grande Minatomirai | 149

60DP type

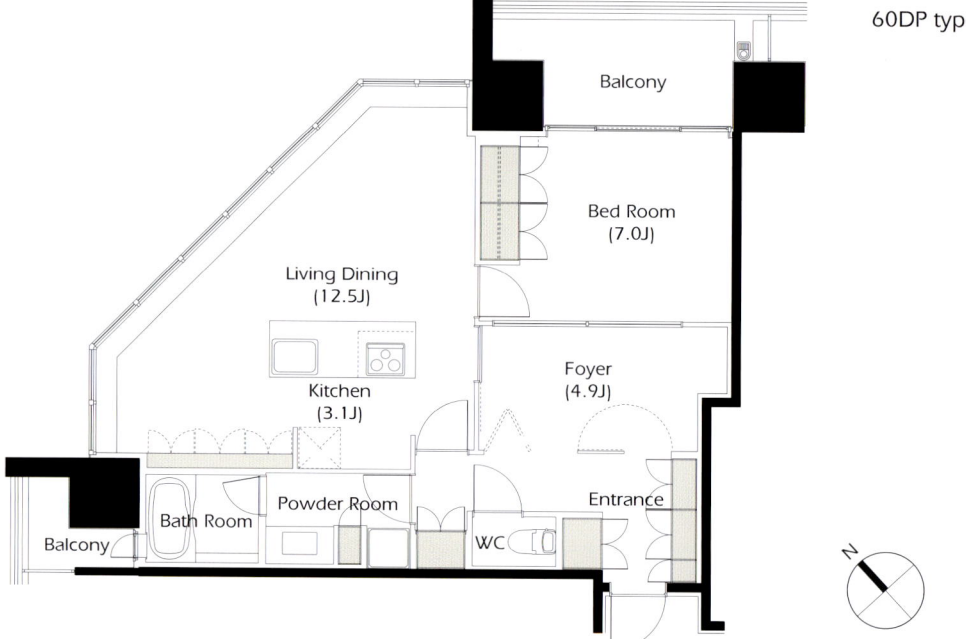

	1	2	
		3	

1
ホワイエ：玄関の扉を開けると、白く輝く鏡面仕上げのタイルを敷き詰めた贅沢な空間が広がる。引き戸や可動間仕切りの採用により、フレキシブルな使い方ができる
Foyer: When one opens the entrance door, one finds oneself in a luxurious space covered with white mirror-finish tiles. Also provided are sliding doors and mobile partitions for flexible use of the space.

2
機能的で洗練されたオールステンレスのキッチン。開放感あふれるアイランド型でリビングとの一体感が心地いい
Sophisticated and fully equipped all stainless kitchen is an island type, giving a sense of integrity with the living room.

3
ワイド&ハイサッシュから自然光が降り注ぐリビング・ダイニング
Sunlight washes the living-dining space through the wide and high saches.

みなとみらいミッドスクエア・ザ・タワーレジデンス
M.M.MID SQUARE The Tower Residence

ORIX Real Estate Corporation / LAND Co., Ltd. / Tokyu Land Corporation / MITSUI & CO., LTD.
Eric Lloyd Wright / Tokyu Architects & Engineers / Yosei Kiyono

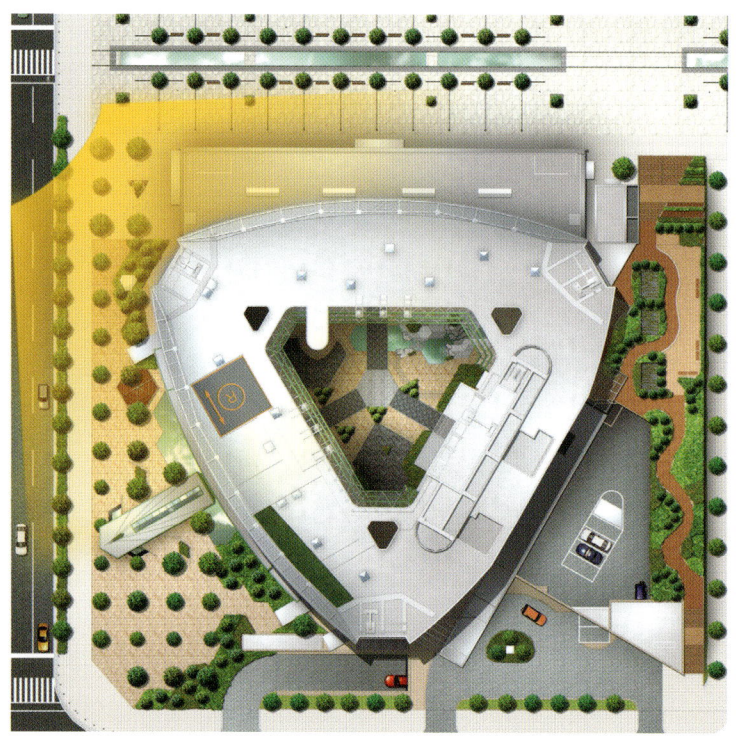

Data

Title
M.M.MID SQUARE The Tower Residence

Developer
ORIX Real Estate Corporation
LAND Co., Ltd.
Tokyu Land Corporation
MITSUI & CO., LTD.

Design Supervision
Eric Lloyd Wright

Architect
Tokyu Architects & Engineers

Sky Lounge Design
Yosei Kiyono

Location
Yokohama city, Kanagawa

Site area
10,151.94m²

Building area
5,338.85m²

Total floor area
82,284.58m²

Structure
RC (S in part)

Completion
June, 2007

Materials
Exterior Wall :
　sprayed coating, tile
Public Wall :
　tile
Public Floor :
　natural stone

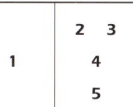

1
エントランスアプローチ：ステンドグラスの天窓はエリック・ロイド・ライト氏デザインによるもの。波をモチーフにしたステンドグラスが透過し、海面のゆらぎとなって空間を彩る
Entrance approach: The stained glass skylight windows are designed by Mr. Eric Lloyd Wright. Light coming through the wave-motif stained glass reminds one of the waves on the sea.

2
グランパティオより吹抜けを見上げる。水や緑の潤いだけでなく、高さ100mもの吹抜けが空と大地とを結ぶ
The well looked up from the Grand Patio. This 100-meter-high well rich with trees and water connects the earth and the sky.

3
「集い」の広場、モニュメンタルパーク
The Monumental Park is a gathering place.

4
エレメンタルガーデン
Elemental Garden

5
ゲストルーム：エリック・ロイド・ライト氏デザインによる非日常空間
Guestroom: Mr. Wright designed this extraordinary space.

M.M.MID SQUARE The Tower Residence | 153

外観基壇部のデザイン監修を担当したエリック・ロイド・ライト氏が、そこに求めたもの。それはタワー建築が忘れがちな、温もりと優しさ、風合いと素材感。遠くから眺める際には、ランドマークとして誇れる存在感も大切かもしれない。しかし帰り着く人々の視点に立ったとき欠かすことができないのは、心を柔らかにしてくれる安らぎではないだろうか。メインエントランス周辺に森を創り、プライベートな時間へと穏やかに切り替えてゆくという発想も、エリック氏によるもの。上質な素材、手の込んだ細工を施したデザイン柱やステンドグラスなど、妥協を知らない細部へのこだわりが超高層建築の威圧感を抑え、住み継がれる邸宅の顔にふさわしい重厚感を深めている。綿密な都市デザイン計画のガイドラインに基づき、一体感のある美しい街づくりを進める、みなとみらい。その街並に調和するよう、白を基調としたデザインとしている。コーナーには床から天井まで続くカーテンウォールを採用。南から降りそそぐ太陽の光、大きなガラス面に映し出される空の表情が、天へ伸びる垂直ラインに生命力を与えシンボリックな力強さを生み出す。上層部に向かうにつれルーバーはガラス手すりへと変化し、建物が大空へ少しずつ溶け込んでゆくかのように演出。最頂部を縁取るアクセントデザインは夜にはライトアップされ、遠景におけるシンボルとして視線を集めるだろう。

What Mr. Eric Lloyd Wright in charge of the exterior design of the podium of the tower requires in this building is a sense of warmth, gentleness, texture, and materials often forgotten in high-rise building designs. When it is viewed from a distance, its presence as a landmark may be more or less important. But when we stand on the viewpoint of the residents returning home, the most important thing is probably a feeling of comfort to caress their hearts. Also from Mr. Wright is the idea to create a forest near the main entrance for a gradual and slow transition to a private time. Uncompromising attention to details such as quality materials, designed columns elaborately worked on and stained glasses results in a reduced sense of oppressive presence inherent to skyscrapers and a deepened feeling of dignity suitable for the facade of the residences to be succeeded from generation to generation.

In Minatomirai, detailed urban design planning guidelines has realized an integrated urban town planning with consistency. To match the townscape, the building is designed on the basis of the color of white. At the corners of the buildings are curtain walls rising up from the floor to the ceiling. Rich sunlight from the south and the changing colors of the sky reflected on the large glass walls give a symbolic sense of strength and vitality to the vertical lines of the building rising into the sky. Toward the top of the tower, louvers are gradually replaced by glass railings, producing an impression as if the building melts into the heaven step by step. The design highlighting the top of the tower is illuminated at night and is expected to attract attention as the symbol of the building when seen from the distance.

| 1 |
| 2 |
| 3 |

1 - 3
フランク・ロイド・ライトのデザインソースを随所に散りばめたスカイラウンジ。天然素材を多用することで、自然との共生を提唱するライト家の思想を反映している

The sky lounge is characterized by many design idioms of Mr. Wright. Utilization of natural materials reflects his family's philosophy proposing the coexistence with the nature.

リラクシング・モード
Relaxing Mode

1
ダイニングからリビングを臨む
The living space seen from the living area

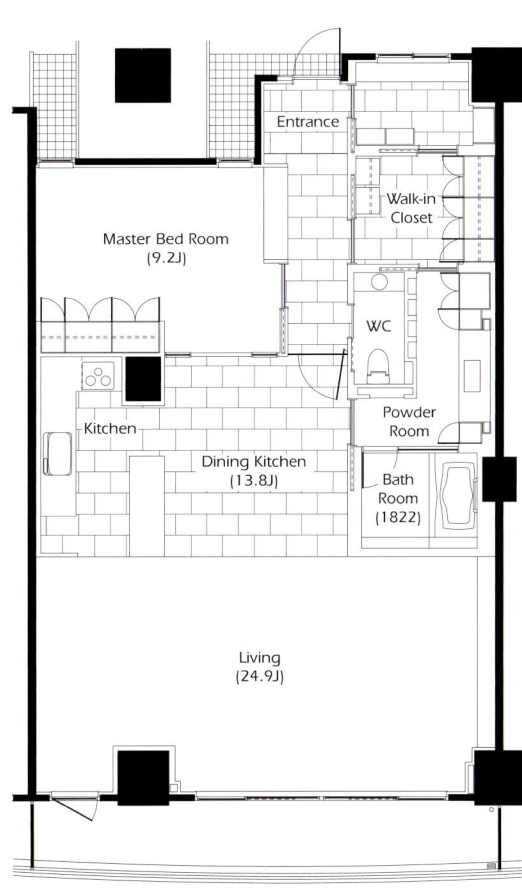

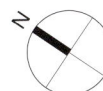

Data

Title
　RELAXING MODE

Area
　114.29m²

Materials
　Interior Wall :
　　natural stone, vinyl cloth
　Interior Floor :
　　natural stone, flooring, carpet

M.M.MID SQUARE The Tower Residence | 155

1	2
	3
	4

1
大理石を敷き詰めた気品溢れる玄関ホール
The elegant entrance hall is floored with marble.

2
ガラスのディスプレイ棚越しにマスターベッドルームを臨む
The master bedroom seen through the glass display shelves

3
リビング・ダイニングルーム
The living-dining room

4
アーティスティックな雰囲気をもった約24.9畳の広さが使い方の可能性を広げる、ゆとりのリビングルーム
The spacious living room with an artistic atmosphere is as wide as 40 square meters and offers flexibility of use.

ここは、光が遊ぶ住まい。最上階ソレイユタイプのみに許された、天からの恵みを享受するプラン。コントラストの強いインテリアの中に降り注ぐ、トップライトからの自然光は、昼に柔らかな陽光を、夜には妖艶な月の光を誘い込み、空間の印象を変えてゆく。趣味の時間に浸る時、本来の自分を取り戻す時。刻一刻と移り変わるその多彩な表情は、ライフシーンをドラマティックな一幕へと誘う。

This is a unit where lights play. This luxury is only available for the Soleil Plan at the top of the tower, allowing residents to fully enjoy the light from the sky. Natural light is invited in the interior highly contrasted in design from the toplight. Soft sunlight in daytime and bewitching moonlight at night always give the space different impressions. Its myriad of expressions changing over time makes the residents' scenes of tower life.

1	2	3
	4	
	5	

1
天井から自然光を採り入れられるトップライト（天窓）を採用したソレイユタイプならではの贅沢。陽の下で食事が愉しめるリゾースティックな独立型ダイニング
This luxury of toplight to let natural light in from the ceiling is unique to the Soleil type units. This separate dining area reminds one of a resort where one can enjoy food under the sun.

2
高級感のある天然石を使用したキッチン
The kitchen uses natural stone giving a sense of quality.

3
玄関近くに配されたウォークインクロゼット。余裕の収納量を確保している
This walk-in closet is set up near the entrance. Its capacity is sufficient enough to store large amounts of clothing.

4
壁面に大型のシステム収納を設けた約9.2畳のワイドなマスターベッドルーム。くつろぎを大切にしたスペース
This 15-square-meter master bedroom has a large storage unit on the wall, emphasizing a sense of relaxation.

5
風合いが美しい天然石仕上げの浴室
The bathroom is finished with natural stone having a beautiful texture.

E.L. ライト モデル
E.L. WRIGHT MODEL
Eric Lloyd Wright

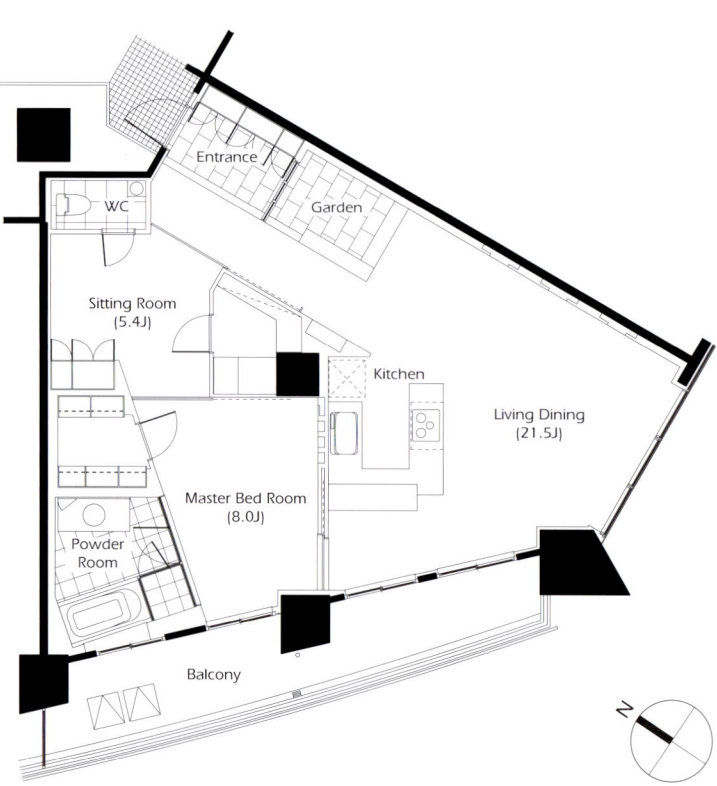

「オーガニックアーキテクチャー」の建築哲学に基づき、エリック・ロイド・ライト氏によってデザインされたプラン。全体をひと続きの空間としながら、ステンドグラスやスライドドアの採用により視界の遮断と空間の連続を同居。自然との共存を感じさせるインサイドガーデンや壁一面の木質パネル、天然石を使用した浴室など、各所に散りばめられた自然の風合いが、目まぐるしい時間を過ごす日常の中に、落ち着いた心を取り戻させてくれる。

Based on the architectural philosophy of "Organic Architecture," Mr. Wright designed this plan. All the spaces are integrated into one, but by employment of stained glass and sliding doors, made compatible are blocked-off lines of sight and continuity of spaces. Natural textures found in a variety of places including the "inside garden" suggesting coexistence with nature, wooden panels fully covering the walls and the bathroom using natural stone enable one to regain a sense of comfort and relaxation in high-paced everyday life.

1
ダイニング・キッチン：植物の呼吸、木目のリズム、全てが調和する幻想的秩序が感じられる
Dining room-cum-kitchen: This space has a fantastic order where breaths of plants, rhythms of wood grain and everything else seem to be in harmony with each other.

Data
Title
　E.L. WRIGHT MODEL
Designer / Architect
　Eric Lloyd Wright
Area
　88.69m²
Materials
　Interior Wall :
　　natural stone, wood panel
　　vinyl cloth, stained glass
　Interior Floor :
　　natural stone, flooring, carpet

1	
2	
3	4

1
インサイドガーデン：大谷石で囲った潤いのグリーンスペース。オーガニックアーキテクチャーの象徴

Inside Garden: This small space to enjoy green is surrounded by Oya tuff stone, symbolizing the organic architecture.

2
すべての空間へと回遊できるさわやかな光溢れるリビング。随所に和のテイストが取り入れられている

The living space rich in light leads up to every other spaces of the unit. Design in Japanese taste can be found everywhere.

3
みなとみらいの眺望と一体感が愉しめる御影石を用いた浴室と洗面室。広がりのある全面ガラス貼り

The bathroom and the washroom using granite offers a magnificent view of Mina-tomirai, letting one feel as if one were integral part of the area. It is fully glass walled to give a sense of expansion.

4
和の趣が感じられる落ち着いた雰囲気のベッドルーム

This bedroom with a sense of Japanese elegance has a comfortable atmosphere.

是空同心
ZEQUE DOSHIN
O.M.CORPORATION / Tadashi Suga

SITE PLAN / 1F PLAN

TYPICAL FLOOR PLAN

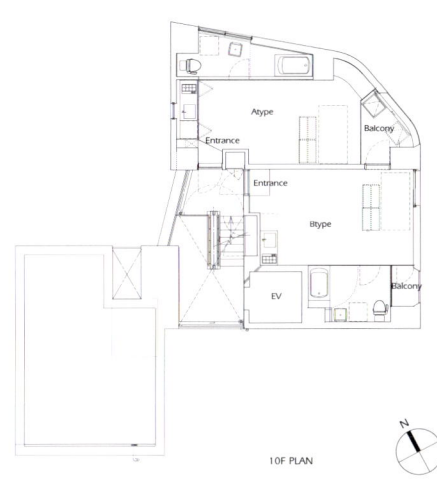
10F PLAN

Data

Title
Zeque Doshin

Developer
O.M.CORPORATION

Architect
Tadashi Suga

Location
Kita-ku, Osaka city

Site area
140.95m²

Building area
112.73m²

Total floor area
1,029.7m²

Area
28.01-29.42m²

Structure
RC

Completion
March, 2006

Materials
Exterior Wall :
 urethane painting
Public Wall :
 architectural concrete

Materials
Public Floor :
 scrubbed finishing ballast
Interior Wall :
 architectural concrete
Interior Floor :
 ceramic tile

Photo
Yoshiharu Matsumura

この建物は賃貸ワンルームマンションである。場所は帝国ホテルの北の比較的近くに位置しながらも、下町的な雰囲気をもつ場所にある。敷地は角ばったひょうたん型で建築法規上、施工上、高度な設計作業を必要とした。この建物の場合、通常の四角の敷地に建つケースと違い、当然建築費はかなり割高になることを施主も理解した上での事業になる。地方都市においては、首都圏ほどは高くはない家賃で収益性をある程度確保する必要がある。そのためには意匠性も含めた合理的判断が資産性も左右する。つまり規模はどうしようもないので、躯体コストを下げることが重要になる。高いレンタブルを実現しながら、バランスよく意匠性も考えられた。そのひとつとしてファサードを一つのスクリーンとして考え、意匠性と遮音性を併せ持つ。プランは敷地形状の複雑さとは反比例して、比較的オーソドックスではあるが、施主からの条件の中において、空間の効率性を限界まで引き出している。

This building accommodates studio units for rent. Though it is located in the north of and comparatively near the Imperial Hotel, the neighborhood has an old-quarter-like atmosphere. The site is gourd-shaped and with angular sides when seen from the top and required highly sophisticated design works. The project was implemented with the understanding by the owner that the construction cost would be much higher than that of buildings built on a normal rectangular site. In local cities, it is necessary to secure profit to some extent with house rents not as high as those of the metropolitan area. The building's asset value depends on a rational approach including designs. In other words, as the designer could do nothing about the scale of the structure, it was important to reduce the building frame cost. While demonstrating a high rentability, the building is designed with a good balance. One of the ideas is to grasp the facade as a screen with priority on both design and sound insulation. In spite of the irregular shape of the site, the plan is rather orthodox but takes optimal advantage of the spatial efficiency while satisfying the client's requirements.

1
B type：玄関方向を見る
B type: Seen from the entrance

1
C type：北よりキッチン方向を見る
C type: Toward the kitchen seen from the north

2
A type：東よりキッチン方向を見る
A type: Toward the kitchen seen from the east

3
A type：トイレ方向を見る
A type: Toward the toilet

キャナルファーストタワー
Canal First Tower

MARUBENI Corporation / KOWA REAL ESTATE CO., LTD. / Urban Corporation
Yasuhiro Hamano / OBAYASHI CORPORATION

都心ならではの利便性を享受しながら、心地よい住環境も満喫できる未来居住街区「東雲キャナルコート」。総開発面積約16.4ha、総計画個数約6000戸。各界のオピニオンリーダーから提案されたイメージを基に、都心居住の新たなモデル都市が創造されている。「東雲キャナルコート」という美しい街に、豊かな緑の存在をプラスした「キャナルファーストタワー」は、おだやかな運河を望む上質な最前席となる。「東雲」とは「夜明け、あけぼの」という意味。その昔、住居の明かり取りに使用されていた篠竹の編み目が明るくなることから「篠の目」と呼ばれるようになったとか。古今和歌集にも詠まれている、なんとも趣のある言葉。「キャナルファーストタワー」の意匠を個性的なものにしているのは、その"東雲色"。朝焼けに染まる雲の色から名付けられた、日本古来の伝統色。この東雲色のラインをアクセントとすることで、無機質になりがちなタワーマンションのデザインを、ぬくもりのある表情に仕上げている。美しく澄んだ青空、おだやかに流れる運河の水面。そして、タワーの足元を包み込むのは、「東雲水辺公園」と連なる豊かな緑。空と青と大地の緑が印象的な風景に、優美なスカイラインを描く。

The Shinonome Canal First Court is a future-oriented residential district enabling its residents to enjoy convenience of living at the heart of the city as well as comfortable living environments. The total area of development is as wide as about 16.4 hectares, and the total number of units reaches about 6,000. Based on the ideas proposed by opinion leaders of different fields, this new town is created to serve as a model of city center residence. Enjoying the combination of the beautiful town of the Shinonome Canal Court and the rich green, the Canal First Tower is the best vantage point to view the gently flowing canal.

Shinonome means a "dawn" or "sunrise." In ancient Japan, Sasamorpha borealis (shino-dake) was knitted (ami-me) and used for transom windows. When a dawn came, the sunlight would come through this amime, and thus they started to call it "shino no me." This elegant word is even found in the Collection of Ancient and Modern Japanese Poetry compiled back in the 10th century. What makes the design of the Canal First Tower unique is its "shinonome iro" or color of the dawn. It is a traditional Japanese color named after the color of clouds outlined in red by the early morning sun. By taking advantage of the lines in this color to accentuate its outlines, this high-rise building that might otherwise become expressionless is designed to give a sense of warmth. Surrounding the building are a beautiful and clear blue sky, slowly running water in the canal, and the rich green at the foot of the tower continuing from the "Shinonome Waterfront Park." The building creates an elegant skyline in the urban landscape with impressive colors of the blue sky and green gardens.

Data

Title	**Location**	**Materials**
Canal First Tower	Koto-ku, Tokyo	Exterior Wall :
Developer	**Site area**	tile
MARUBENI Corporation	6448.16m²	Public Wall :
KOWA REAL ESTATE CO., LTD.	**Area**	stone, tile
Urban Corporation	90C TYPE 96.17m²	Public Floor :
Design Supervision	70A TYPE 70.71m²	stone, flooring
Yasuhiro Hamano	**Structure**	Interior Wall :
Architect	RC	vinyl cloth
OBAYASHI CORPORATION	**Completion**	Interior Floor :
	February, 2008	tile, flooring

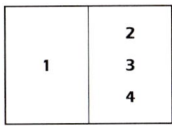

1
プリズムコート：ウッドデッキが気持ちいい中庭
Prism Court: The patio with a comfortable wood deck.

2
敷地内に大きな水盤置くことで、運河との連続性を高めたアクアガーデン
In the Aqua Garden, the presence of a large pool on the site enhances a sense of continuity with the canal.

3
壁面いっぱいに広がる一大パノラマを楽しむ、2層吹き抜けのアークホール
The 2-story-high Arc Hall offers a panoramic view from full-wall windows.

4
BREEZE（ブリーズ）：水のある風景を楽しみながら、フォーマルなパーティを楽しめる本格的なパーティルーム
BREEZE: Offering a scene with rippling water, this fully equipped party room can be used for formal parties.

90C-TYPE

ZENな時間を楽しむ、大人のLOHAS空間。欧米で人気の高い「ZEN」スタイル。それは、シンプルな空間の中に豊かさを発見し、和のテイストをモダンに昇華すること。伸びやかに広がるリビング・ダイニング。深みのあるブラウンを基調としたカラーコーディネート。そして琉球畳をあしらった板の間が、一枚の絵のように空間全体を引き締める。真のやすらぎを追求した、上質な時間がここにある。

90C-TYPE

This unit type is intended to be a LOHAS (Lifestyles of Health and Sustainability) space for adults to enjoy Zen-inspiring hours. The "Zen" style now popular in the West means finding richness in a simple space and modernize the traditional Japanese taste. The living-dining space is designed to be spacious. Color coordination is based on the color of deep brown. The wooden floor with Ryukyu tatami mats gives a sense of depth to the unit as if it were a painted picture. One will find quality time in pursuit of true comfort.

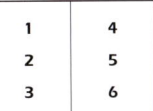

1
90C-Type リビング・ダイニング・キッチン：自然のぬくもりを感じる心地よい空間
90C-TYPE: This living room and a dining room-cum-kitchen is a comfortable space giving a sense of warmth of nature.

2
90C-Type 和室と一体化した伸びやかなリビング・ダイニング
90C-TYPE: The spacious living-dining area is integrated with the Japanese-style room.

3
90C-Type 琉球畳をあしらった上質な和室。リビングと一体となり空間を引き締めている
90C-TYPE: Quality Japanese-style room with Ryuku tatami mats. One with the living space, it gives a sense of integrity of the space.

4
90C-Type キャプション
90C-TYPE: Kitchen

5
90C-Type 落ち着いた雰囲気のベッドルーム
90C-TYPE: Well-lit and clean Western-style room

6
70A-Type 格納できるキッチンによってフレキシブルな空間が生まれる
70A -TYPE: The retractable kitchen unit contributes to flexibility of the space.

70A-TYPE

自分らしい感性で、生活そのものを楽しむ、モダンなプライベートスイート。"透明感"をテーマにセレクトされた、洗練されたインテリア。ホワイトを基調にした、モダンなカラーコーディネート。そして、キッチンを格納することで生まれる、空間のフレキシビリティー。まるで上等な生成りのシャツのような、シンプルで美しいライフスタイルの提案。

70A-TYPE

This modern, private suite is for those who enjoy living on their own sensitivities. The sophisticated interior is on the theme of a "sense of transparency." The color coordination is based on white, giving a modern impression. The space offers flexibility, thanks to the retractable kitchen unit. The unit offers a simple and beautiful lifestyle, reminding one of an unbleached quality shirt.

1
70A-Type 心地良い雰囲気のリビング・ダイニング。透明ガラスの奥にベッドルームを配している
70A-Type: The living-dining area has a comfortable atmosphere. The bedroom is behind the transparent glass.

2
70A-Type リビングからガラスのパーティションで仕切られたダイニングとキッチンを臨む
70A-TYPE: The dining space and the glass-partitioned kitchen seen from the living room.

3
70A-Type ゆったりとしたベッドルーム。透明ガラスで仕切られているため、空間に広がりを感じる
70A-TYPE: Partitioned by the transparent glass, this roomy bedroom gives a sense of spaciousness.

SYOQUE MINATOMACHI

匠空 MINATOMACHI
Syoque Minatomachi
O.M.CORPORATION
Kiyoshi Ishibashi Architect & Associates / Kiyoshi Ishibashi

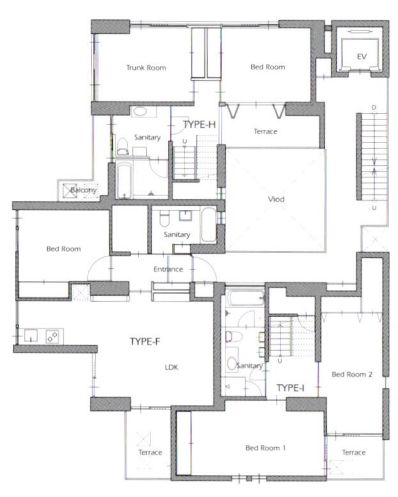

9 F PLAN

10F PLAN

1
白を基調とした室内。天井高は2700
This unit has a white-based interior and enjoys the ceiling height of 2,700mm.

Data

Title
Syoque Minatomachi

Developer
O.M.CORPORATION

Designer / Architect
Kiyoshi Ishibashi Architect & Associates
Kiyoshi Ishibashi

Location
Naniwa-ku, Osaka city

Site area
272.56m²

Building area
243.23m²

Total floor area
1660.43m²

Area
36.00-138.09m²

Structure
RC

Completion
December, 2005

Materials
Exterior Wall :
 50x50 tile, water- repellent
 coating on architectural concrete
Public Wall :
 50x50 tile, water- repellent coating
 on architectural concrete

Materials
Public Floor :
 tile
Interior Wall :
 EP
Interior Floor :
 tile

Photo
Yoshiharu Matsumura

この建物は、大阪市のJR難波駅から至近距離の交通至便な地に位置している。敷地東側に湊町リバープレイスが建ち、北側には道頓堀川が流れ、流行のカフェやショップが軒を連ねる堀江へも徒歩圏内で、都市生活を満喫できる最適な環境である。1、2階を店舗、3〜10階を住戸としている。住戸は1LDKを基本としており、最上部2層は2〜3LDKのメゾネットタイプで構成されている。住戸へは敷地北側の露地的雰囲気のエントランス階段を上がり、2階の住戸エントランスホールからアクセスする。住戸階では、エレベーターを降りるとガラスで覆われたライトコート（光庭）が現れ、降り注ぐ光とスリットから運ばれる風が、居住者の気分を新鮮なものにしてくれる。室内は稜線を整理し、シンプルで使い勝手のよい空間としている。天井高さは2700を確保している。水廻りはユニットバスを用いず、在来工法の浴槽を用いており、五感を満足させる癒しの雰囲気をつくっている。また最上部2層のメゾネットタイプでは、広い屋外テラスを設け、邸宅的な感覚を演出し、グレードを高めている。全戸において屋内と屋外が一体的に楽しめるように配慮をしている。道路に面しない住戸はライトコート（光庭）に面しており、開放感とプライバシー確保を両立した心地よい空気感を十分に味わえる。都市に住む便利さ、快適性に加えて、感性を刺激する豊かさが住み手には味わってもらえるものと自負している。

Close to the JR Namba Station in Osaka, this building is favorably located in terms of transportation. To the east of the site is the Minatomachi River Place, and to the north runs the Dotonbori River. Horie where fashionable cafe terraces and shops stand side by side is in a walking distance. The site offers the best environment to enjoy city life. All the floors of this 10-story building provide residential units apart from the first and second floors that accommodate shops and stores. Most of the units have one bedroom and a living room with a combined dining room and kitchen (LDK), and maisonnette type units of two or three bedrooms plus an LDK are available on the top two floors. To the north of the site is the stairway in a back alley-like atmosphere, leading up to the entrance hall on the second floor for access to the units. When one gets off the elevator, one finds an impressive light court enclosed in glass walls and feels refreshed by the pouring light and winds through the slits. The interior has simplified edge lines for creating a simple and convenient space. The ceiling is as high as 2,700mm. For the bathroom, a conventional bathtub is employed in place of a unit bath, enabling one to take a relax in a carefully designed bathroom. Each maisonnette type residence on the top two floors has a wide outdoor terrace, giving a detached house-like atmosphere and a sense of high grade. In all the units, due consideration is made for the interior and the exterior to enable residents to enjoy them as one. The units not facing the road faces the light court instead, and one can fully enjoy a comfortable atmosphere having both a sense of freedom and privacy. We are sure that this design enables residents to enjoy richness stimulating their sensitivities in addition to convenience and comfort of living in a city.

1	2
3	
4	5

1
東面道路より住戸エントランスを見る
The entrance to the units seen from the road to the east

2
路地的雰囲気の住戸エントランス階段
The entrance stairway to the units has a back alley-like atmosphere.

3
シンプルで使い勝手のよいLDK
This living room with a combined dining room and kitchen (LDK) is simple and easy-to-use.

4
明るい光にあふれる寝室
The bedroom is filled with pouring light.

5
寝室とLDKを仕切るガラススクリーンと格子戸
The glass screen and the lattice door separate the bedroom and the LDK.

1	2
3	
4	

1
黒のタイルを効果的に用いた水廻り
The bathroom and washing room effectively use black tiles.

2
ゆとりのあるキッチン
Spacious kitchen

3
ライトコート（光庭）と一体になるLDK
LDK integrated with the light court

4
最上階メゾネットタイプの屋上テラス
The roof terrace of the maisonette type unit on the top floor

HUQUE Building Minamisemba

HUQUE building MINAMISEMBA
HUQUE building MINAMISEMBA
Fukuhara Kogyo / Hiroyuki Wakabayashi

Data

Title
HUQUE building MINAMISEMBA

Developer
Fukuhara Kogyo

Architect
Hiroyuki Wakabayashi

Location
Chuo-ku, Osaka city

Site area
527.36m²

Building area
478.25m²

Total floor area
3815.03m²

Area
33.01-61.54m²

Structure
S (SRC in part)

Completion
April, 2004

Materials
Exterior Wall :
  lundex-coat on architectural concrete
  color lundex-coat on extrusion
  cement board
  hot dip galvanizing expanded metal
Public Wall :
  glass mosaic tile
  lundex-coat on architectural concrete
Public Floor :
  granite (jet burner finish)
Interior Wall :
  vinyl cloth on PB
Interior Floor :
  flooring

Photo
Yoshiharu Matsumura

	2	3
1	4	5

1
南側外観：日中、太陽光による陰影が刻々と変化する。エキスパンドメタルは溶融亜鉛メッキ素地仕上
Southern exterior: Shading by the sunlight continuously changes throughout the daytime. The expanded metal is finished with hot-dip galvanizing.

2
西側外観：躯体打ち込みの丸鋼60φがダブルスキンを支持する。直通部の開口は非常用進入口
Western exterior: 60mm round bars embedded into the skeleton support the double-skin structure. The openings on the sides of the straight way are emergency entrances.

3
西側夜景：メッシュの輪郭線は光に置き変わる
Western exterior at night: Lights replace the meshed contours.

4
マンションエントランス：夕景
Entrance to the building in the evening

5
ショップエントランス：夕景
Shop entrance in the evening

南船場は、若い世代による実験的な店舗が集まりだしたことをきっかけに、最近では多くのブランドショップが進出し、新しい位置付けの商業ゾーンとして脚光をあびている地域である。上層部に計画されたワンルームはSOHO仕様とし、ロフトを備えた開放的な佇まいをめざした。設計当初からの課題は、建築の外壁が持ち得る商業的公共性を生かしつつも、いかに他業種の混在をまとめ、ビルとしての一体感を演出するかということであった。無防備なスケルトンの周囲にグレーチングのキャットウォークを走らせ、さらにエキスパンドメタルの被膜で特徴的にダブルスキンを形成する。テナントの自己主張は、ロゴサイン、ネオン管、又は映像へと姿を変えて、メッシュの内より溢れ出す。この中間領域とも呼べる空間は、外装の維持管理を容易にするだけではなく、ファサード全体を建築の導入部として機能させることに成功している。

Minamisenba is now in the limelight as a new type of commercial zone because many brand shops have recently been opened in the area, triggered by those experimental shops and stores by young generations. The studios planned on the higher stories are SOHO-ready and, provided with lofts, are designed to give an open atmosphere. The challenge from the beginning of the design has been how to produce a sense of integrity as a building accommodating a mixture of different businesses while taking advantage of the commercially public nature of the exterior walls of the building. For this goal, grating catwalks are provided around the unprotected skeleton, and a unique double-skin facade is produced by covering with expanded metal. The self-assertion by the tenants is transformed into their logo signs, neon tubes or video images, flowing out of the mesh. This space that we may call as "intermediate zone" successfully makes the entire facade function as an introduction to the building while making management and maintenance of the exterior easier.

1
2
3

1
LD1
LD1

2
LD2
LD2

3
LD3
LD3

Oazo Ashiya

OAZO ASHIYA
OAZO ASHIYA
Masayuki Tanaka · godai / Tadashi Suga

2.3F PLAN

4F PLAN

5F PLAN

Data

Title
　Oazo Ashiya

Developer
　Masayuki Tanaka · godai

Architect
　Tadashi Suga

Location
　Ashiya city, Hyogo

Site area
　320.58m²

Building area
　224.20m²

Total floor area
　978.42m²

Area
　29.68-72.42m²

Structure
　RC

Completion
　June, 2006

Materials
　Exterior Wall :
　　urethane painting
　Public Wall :
　　architectural concrete
　Public Floor :
　　wood deck
　Interior Wall :
　　architectural concrete
　Interior Floor :
　　cork tile

Photo
　Yoshiharu Matsumura

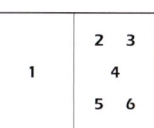

1
外観夜景：壁面後退、高さ制限の厳しいエリアではあるが、だからこそ躍動感がある方が良いと考えた
Exterior at night: As strict regulations on setback and height are imposed, giving a sense of dynamism is thought to be preferable.

2
エントランス方向を見る
Toward the entrance

3
共用廊下を見る。ウッドデッキが内部へ連続している
The public corridor. The wood deck continues on into the interior.

4
LDKを見る
Living room and a dining room-cum-kitchen

5
メゾネット内部階段
The stairway to the maisonnette

6
水廻りの上部トップライト
Toplight above the bathroom

賃貸の共同住宅である。場所は芦屋市の住宅街へ繋がる道の入り口に位置し、廻りも緑豊かなエリアである。しかし、その割には華やかさに欠け、地味な印象であったこともあり、コンサルからの要望は強く印象付けるようなダイナミックさと収益性をあわせ持つことであった。賃貸住宅なので、意匠的にも限界があるうえに、高さ制限、壁面後退など厳しい規制もあり、平面的には明確なコンセプトと効率を優先し、エレベーションで躍動感をつくることを考えた。まず、平面的には賃貸ワンルームの欠点であるチープさを軽減するために水廻りを一体化し、一つの部屋をつくり、共用部はウッドデッキからそのまま非日常的な玄関戸を通り、内部に連続し更に、バルコニーまで連続させた。そのレベルで繋がるデッキから200ミリ下がりでコルクタイルの洋室がある。外観については夜景が判りやすいが、なんとなく閉塞てきな印象の道路との関係を意識し、建っているよりは、置かれている形がダイナミックで美しいと考えた。

This apartment building is located on the corner of the street leading to a residential block in Ashiya City and in a neighborhood rich in green. In spite of such favorable conditions, the site appeared unimpressive and inconspicuous. For this reason, the consultant requested to design a building with dynamism to highly attract people's attention as well as profitability. The fact that the building accommodates rental apartments posed limitations on design while the building height, setback and other strict regulations were imposed. Taking these into consideration, we put priority to presentation of a definitive concept and realization of efficiency in terms of the plan while elevation was taken advantage of to give a sense of dynamism. In order to reduce a sense of cheapness often found with studios for rent, the kitchen and bathroom are integrated into a single room, and the common space offers a sense of continuity from the wood deck outside through the extraordinary door and the interior to the balcony. 200mm down from the level of the deck is a Western-style room floored with cork tiles. As for the exterior design, as more clearly seen in the night view, we put emphasis on an impression that the structure is put rather than built, considering it should be more dynamic and beautiful in contrast with the road that appears rather blocked.

| 1 |
| 2 |
| 3 |

1
共用廊下、内部インナーバルコニーとウッドデッキが連続している
The public corridor, inner balcony and wood deck are all connected.

2
リビング・ダイニング方向を見る
Toward the living room and the dining area

3
インナーバルコニーと同じように水廻りもBOX状になっている
The wet area is boxed as is the case with the inner balcony

北野アパート
Apartment Kitano
Wadakohsan Corporation / Tadashi Suga

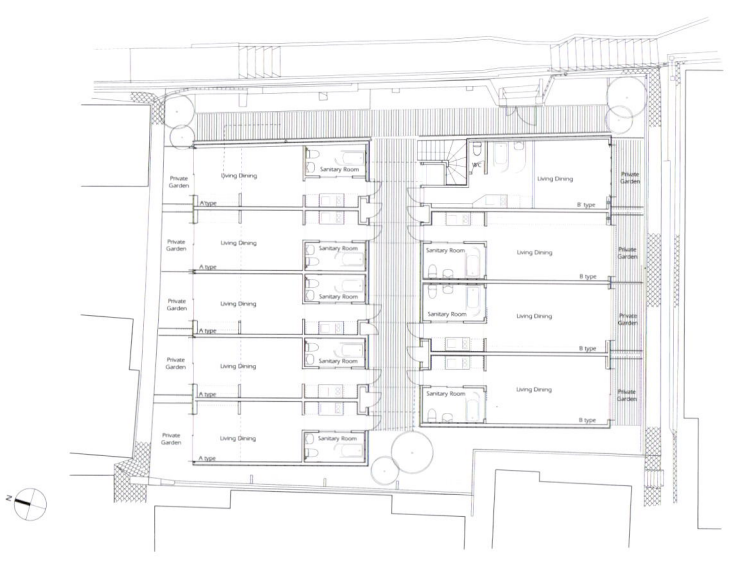

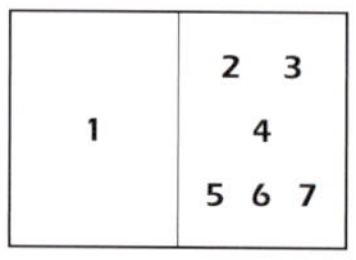

	2	3	
1		4	
	5	6	7

1
木製ルーバーの外皮に覆われた東側ファサード。境界塀越しに中廊下を臨む
The eastern facade covered with an outer skin of wooden louvers. The middle corridor can be seen beyond the bordering wall.

2
1F中廊下を見る。共用廊下はデッキが続く
The middle corridor on the first floor. A series of decks is above the public corridor.

3
2F中廊下を見る。北側住戸へはブリッヂを介してアプローチする
The middle corridor on the second floor. Access to the northern units is via bridges.

4
西側上方より勾配屋根を見る
The sloped roofs seen from the above from the west

5
2F南側住戸内観:白い天井にポツ窓が並ぶ
Interior of the southern unit on the second floor: Small windows are on the ceiling.

6
1F南側住戸内観:内部の床が専用庭デッキと連続する
Interior of the southern unit on the first floor: The interior floor continues to the exclusive garden deck.

7
2F北側住戸内観:天窓から光が注ぐ
Interior of the northern unit on the second floor: Light is pouring from the toplight.

Data

Title
Apartment Kitano

Developer
Wadakohsan Corporation

Architect
Tadashi Suga

Location
Kobe city, Hyogo

Site area
489.83m²

Building area
277.58m²

Total floor area
496.85m²

Area
25.02-33.01m²

Structure
wooden structure

Completion
May, 2006

Materials
Exterior Wall
: wooden louver
Public Wall
: AEP on PB (t=12)

Materials
Public Floor
: wooden deck
Interior Wall
: siding
Interior Floor
: flooring

Photo
Yoshiharu Matsumura

18戸の木造賃貸ワンルームアパートである。敷地は、神戸有数の観光スポットである北野町のほぼ中心に位置する。周囲には異人館が点在し、景観規制の下、いわゆる異国情緒漂う環境がひろがっている。当然、景観条例、文化財保護条例によって、壁面の保存、壁面後退、高さ、容積制限、屋根形状等厳しい規制が掛かるエリアである。屋根形状までも勾配屋根と決まっている。異人館をはじめ、傾斜屋根の多いこの地にはトンガリ屋根が良く似合うのではと考えた。トンガリをもつノコギリ型の屋根をのせたヴォリュームを二分するようにヴォイドをとり、南と北に住戸を配する構成とした。吹き抜けの中廊下をスキップさせて、下階にも光が届く光庭としている。天窓、高窓、はきだし窓を組み合わせて、どのタイプの住戸もそれぞれ多様な光につつまれるよう意図している。外観は木製のルーバーで覆った。素材の変化とともに年を追って、この街に溶け込んでいくことを期待している。

This is an 18-unit wooden condominium accommodating studio apartments. The site is nearly at the center of Kitano Town, one of the most famous tourist spots in the city of Kobe. Western-style residences are dotted around the site, and under the landscape regulations, a neighborhood that radiates exoticism has been preserved. As the area is subject to the townscape and cultural property conservation ordinances, architectural structures are strictly regulated in terms of wall surface preservation, wall setback, height, bulk regulation, roof shape, etc., and in fact, the sloped roof shape is mandatory. Taking these into consideration, pointed roofs seem to be suitable in the area where many buildings and houses including Western-style ones have sloped roofs. A void is prepared in between the two volumes with pointed and serrated roofs, and the units are located on the north and the south sides of the buildings. The middle corridor in the well is partly roofed by the decks to enable natural light to reach the lower level and serves as a light garden. A combination of skylights, high windows and floor-level windows is intended to provide every type of units with different types of light. The exterior is covered with wooden louvers. It is expected that, along with aging of the materials, the apartment will melt into the townscape.

WK Tamatukuri

WK玉造
WK TAMATUKURI

WaKu fudousan.co., ltd. / ueda tomoharu architects inc.

1
道路側からの見上げ
The facade looked up from the frontal road

Data

Title
WK Tamatukuri

Developer
WaKu fudousan.co., ltd.

Architect
ueda tomoharu architects inc.

Location
Higashinari-ku, Osaka city

Site area
180.17m²

Building area
152.23m²

Total floor area
860.44m²

Area
29.05 ~ m²

Structure
RC

Completion
March, 2006

Materials
Exterior Wall :
 architectural concrete, tile
 fluorine painting
Public Wall :
 architectural concrete
Public Floor :
 ceramic tile
Interior Wall :
 AEP on PB
Interior Floor :
 red pine flooring

Photo
Yoshiharu Matsumura

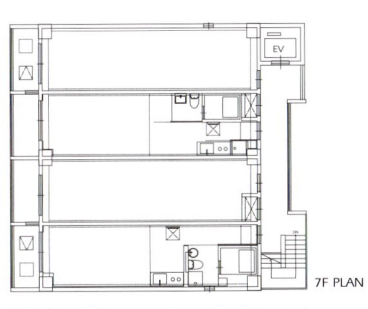
7F PLAN

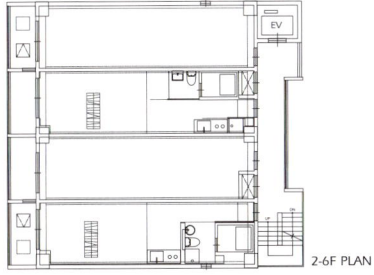
2-6F PLAN

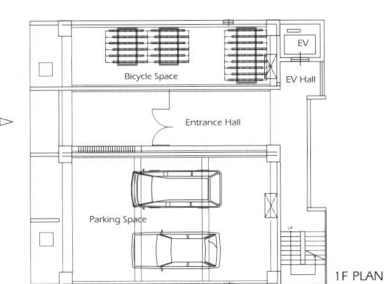
1F PLAN

計画地は、幅員の広い前面道路に面する正方形に近いニュートラルな形状である。建築は、この敷地形状に対してコストをかけず最も有効にボリュームを取り出せるよう敷地がそのまま立ち上がったかのような立方体を2つ重ねた程度のシンプルな箱とした。平面計画についても、まずは一見これ以上ないかのような単純な横割りプランとしておいて、内部空間のなかで唯一、イレギュラーな要素を埋め込む操作を行った。扉ではなく壁がスライドすることによって居室とコネクトする洗面スペースは、閉じた空間としても、居室の一部としても機能するため、床面積以上の広さを体感することが可能だ。あまり意識的に建築デザインをせず、こうした自制を効かした上での反復作業の繰り返し中で、ふとイレギュラーなものを見いだす行為も建築の魅力的なソリューションのひとつといえる。

The site has a neutral, semi-square shape facing a wide frontal road. In order to achieve the maximum floor area while minimizing the cost, the building structure is designed to contain nearly two cubes having a length of the side equivalent to that of the site. As for the floor planning, the utmost simplest plan is first given, and then a single irregular factor is added to the interior space. Not the door but the wall slides to connect the living room and the washing space which serves not only as a closed room but also as part of the living area, making the space appear more spacious than it actually is. It is one of the attractive architectural solutions to find something irregular by chance in a repeated, self-constrained design process, not through strongly conscious efforts.

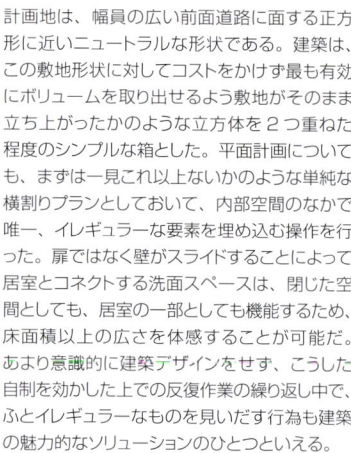

1
上階 住戸ユニットの区画がそのまま連続したエントランスホール
The width of the entrance hall is equivalent to that of the upper floor compartment.

2
エントランスホール見返し
The frontal road looked back from the entrance hall

3
高い天井高を有効に利用した住戸ユニットA
Residential unit A taking advantage of its high ceiling height

4
高い天井高を有効に利用した住戸ユニットB
Residential unit B taking advantage of its high ceiling height

ディナ
DINa
Michio Ohta

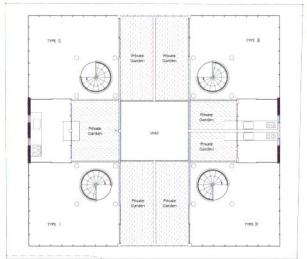

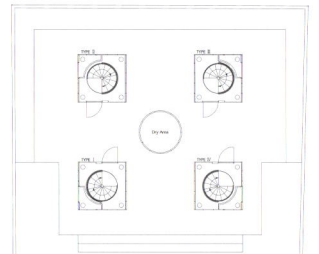

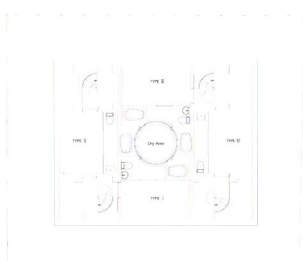

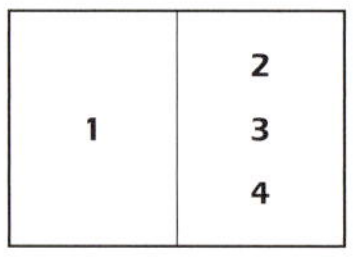

	2
1	3
	4

1
正面外観
Facade

2
2階主室からキッチンを臨む
The kitchen seen from the main room on the second floor

3
2階主室から外室を臨む
The outer space seen from the main room on the second floor

4
ヴォイドからの光がガラスブロックを通して地下室の閉塞感を和らげている
Lights from the void come through the glass blocks, reducing the sense of confinement in the basement.

Data

Title
 DINa
Architect
 Michio Ohta
Location
 Nishinomiya city, Hyogo
Site area
 258.90m²
Building area
 155.18m²
Total floor area
 282.75m²
Area
 64.57-128.97m²

Structure
 S (RC in part)
Completion
 April, 2006
Materials
 Exterior Wall :
  extrusion cement board
  + urethane painting
 Public Wall :
  extrusion cement board
  + urethane painting
 Public Floor :
  natural stone (chopped face)

Materials
 Interior Wall :
  EP on PB (t=12.5)
 Interior Floor :
  linden plywood
Photo
 Yoshiharu Matsumura

単身者もしくはディンクスを想定した賃貸集合住宅の計画である。主たるスペースを地上から持ち上げ、大きなピロティ空間を生み出していること、そして一見して集合住宅と判明できない姿をしていることが計画の特徴になっている。閑静な住宅地に建つことから、建物のボリューム分割を図り5つの箱体で構成した。それぞれの箱体はノイズの少ない外形として雑多なものの表出を避けている。各々のユニットは、ピロティから直接アクセスする長屋形式で独立している。ピロティは、界隈の空間であり道を拡張する空間で、公とも私ともいえる領域になっている。この開放された都市のポケットのような空間は、先の震災の記憶と更地時の開放性を引き継ぐもので、街との積極的な結びつきを求めている。敷地の中央に地下から空に続くヴォイドがくり抜かれ、その周囲に4つのユニットが配された。ヴォイドは光と外気を導き入れる装置であり、内外の密接な関係を生み出す宙の庭である。ユニットの内部は静かな地階、エントランスの1階、開放的な2階という、性格の異なる3つの領域が縦に繋がるワンルームの構成となっている。2階の主室は、全周がガラスで覆われて地上から切り離された空間であることが強調されている。外周のガラスには、光を調整するフィルムが挿入され、行灯の中のように包まれた内部は刻々とその表情を変えてゆく。ヴォイド側にはプライバシーの守られた2つの外室（デッキスペース）があり、拡張された床からヴォイドを介して、視界は空に続いている。

In this project, a condominium for rent is planned, mainly for single person households and DINKS (dual-income-no-kids). The uniqueness of the plan lies in the facts that the main building volume is lifted above ground, creating a large pilotis and that the building has a shape that cannot be identified as a condominium at a glance. As this building is to be built in a quiet residential area, the building volume is divided into five boxes. Each box has a shape with noise minimized so that nothing obtrusive or ostentatious is revealed on its exterior. Each unit in this tenement house has a direct access from the pilotis. The pilotis not only gives a sense of neighborhood but also extends the road, serving as a space both public and private. This open space in the silent corner of the town carries on the memory of the last Earthquake disaster and the sense of openness when the lot was vacant, representing the pursuit of positive connections with the town. A vertical and upward void is made from the underground to the sky at the center of the lot, and four units are deployed around it. The void functions as a device to take in light and outside air and creates a strong connection between the outside and the inside of the building, serving as a garden in the air. Each unit is in fact a studio consists of three vertically connected elements with different characters: the quiet basement, the first floor for entrance and the open second floor. The main room on the second floor is mainly covered with glass panels, emphasizing the fact that the space is separated from the ground. Light-adjusting films are inserted in the glass, and the interior changes its impression as if it were built inside the Japanese traditional paper-covered lamp stand. On the side of the void, two outer rooms (deck spaces) to keep privacy are provided, and the view extends from the extended floor to the sky via the void.

La Wasison Kitano

La Wasison 北野
La Wasison Kitano
Wadakohsan Corporation / Tadashi Suga

1
全面道路より車面を臨む
The steep seen from the frontal road

SITE PLAN / 1F PLAN

Data

Title
La Wasison Kitano

Developer
Wadakohsan Corporation

Architect
Tadashi Suga

Location
Kobe city, Hyogo

Site area
558.27m²

Building area
293.22m²

Total floor area
903.78m²

Area
31.59m²

Structure
RC

Completion
April, 2006

Materials
Exterior Wall :
  urethane painting
Public Wall :
  urethane painting
Public Floor :
  tile
Interior Wall :
  architectural concrete
Interior Floor :
  cork tile

Photo
Yoshiharu Matsumura

28戸のワンルームマンションである。4層の南棟と3層の北棟を2つの階段でつなぐ明快な構成としている。前面道路は軽自動車が何とか侵入可能かどうかという状況にある。中廊下型の住戸配置では往々にして条件の悪くなる北側住戸をバルコニーインの形式とし、南側にバルコニーをとることを可能にした。当然それに面する南棟住戸の開口位置をコントロールするとともに、階段室をアルミルーバーで覆い、バルコニーのプライバシーを確保している。南北いずれの棟もバルコニーをとりこんだマッシブなヴォリューム構成とし、また階段室、基壇部にはルーバーを用いてオブジェクトとしての存在を消去した。住棟部である角をとった愛らしいふたつの形態を浮かび上がらせようとしたものだ。道路から十分にセットバックした双子のヴォリュームは、比較的背の低い周辺環境にもすっぽりはまった佇まいをみせている。いずれ、狭い前面道路において、この貴重なポケットパークのような空間が緑で包まれるころ、建物は背景となり、消え去ることが出来る。

This is a 28-studio condominium and has a simple structure of the 4-story south and 3-story north buildings connected by two corridors. The frontal road is so narrow that only a light vehicle can access. As with the middle corridor type dwelling units, conditions of the northern ones are often unfavorable, so in designing this condominium, the balcony access is provided so that all the units should have balconies facing south. Naturally, careful consideration is paid to the positions of the openings of the southern units facing these balconies, and the stairways are covered by aluminum louvers in order to secure privacy of the units. Both the northern and southern buildings give a sense of massive volume by incorporating the balconies while louvers are employed for the stairways and the podium to hide their presence as objects. The corners of the buildings are beveled to highlight these two lovely outlines. Sufficiently set back from the road, these twin volumes completely fit in the rather low-rise neighborhood. When this precious pocket-park-like space is surrounded by green in future, it will become part of the background and hide its presence.

1	2
3	
4	

1
夜景:全面道路よりエントランスを臨む
Night view: The entrance seen from the frontal road

2
夜景:中廊下よりエントランスを臨む
Night view: The entrance seen from the middle corridor

3
D-type 住戸内観:ダイニングテーブルとしても利用できるアイランド型キッチン
D-type unit interior: This island kitchen can also be used as a dining table.

4
A-type 住戸内観:バルコニーのタイルが内部窓際まで貼られたバルコニータイプ
A-type unit interior: The tiles on the balcony are extended to the inside of the window.

FLEG池尻
FLEG Ikejiri
F.L.E.G. INTERNATIONAL CO., LTD. / Akio Yachida

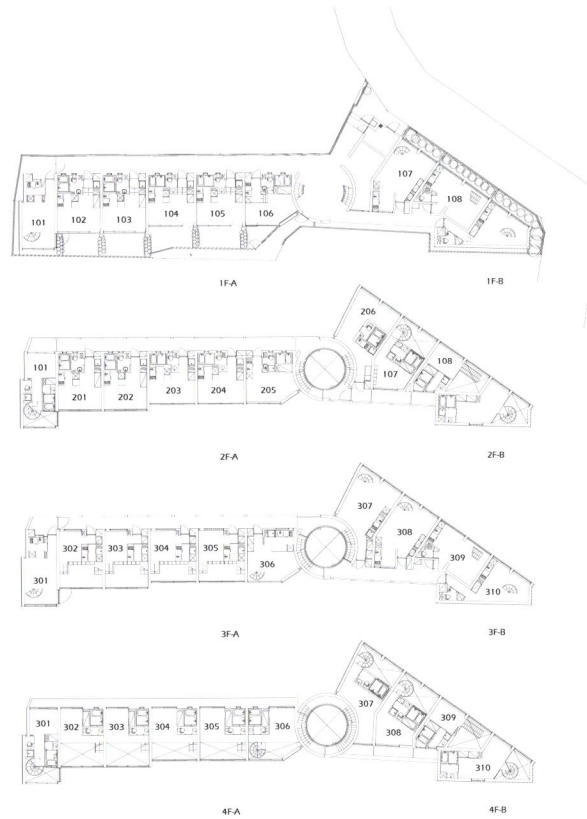

Data

Title
FLEG Ikejiri

Developer
F.L.E.G. INTERNATIONAL CO., LTD.

Architect
Akio Yachida

Location
Setagaya-ku, Tokyo

Area
24.98-59.08m²

Structure
RC

Completion
September, 2005

Materials
Exterior Wall :
 exposed concrete
Public Wall :
Public Floor :
Interior Wall :
 exposed concrete
Interior Floor :
 flooring

コンクリート打ち放しの洗練されたファサード。シリンダー状の壁で囲まれた中庭を中心の広場とし、二重螺旋の階段が天空まで昇りあがることを想起させる。そこにリンクしたリニアな通路から、個の領域へ穏やかに繋がる。各ユニットは大きな開口部のリビングルームがあり、高さに変化を与え、開放的で連続性のある空間としている。素材だけの飾らない仕上げ、敷き詰められた白い床タイルは、都市リビングを異次元の空間へと誘う。自由に空間を使うことにより、暮らしのアイデンティティ（独自性）が高まる。

The sophisticated outer walls of this building are of undressed concrete. The patio surrounded by a cylinder-like wall is positioned as the central square of the lot, reminding one of a double-helix stairway rising up to heaven. The linear passageways linked to the stairway gently lead to individual apartments. Each unit has a living room with a large opening and is provided with different elevations, creating an expansive space with a sense of continuity. Finished to take advantage of the textures of materials and floored with white tiles, this urban living space leads one to another dimension. Allowed to use the space freely, one can build up a stronger identity (or originality) of life.

	2
1	3
	4

1
外観
Facade

2
ダイニングルーム：奥にリビングルームを臨む
The dining room with the living room at the back

3
キッチン
Kitchen

4
ステップフロアになっているため天井が高く開放的なリビングルーム
The living room has a stepped floor, making the ceiling high and giving a sense of openness.

1
リビングルーム・ベットルーム方向を臨む
Living room: Toward the bedroom

2
リビングルーム：階段からの見下ろし
Living room: Looked down from the stairs

3
東西から陽の明かりが射し込む明るいベットルーム
Well-illuminated bedroom bright with lights from the east and west

Sant' Agata

京都市北部、低層の住宅、マンション、商店、寺などが軒を接して混在するエリアに建つ、3階建て11戸の集合住宅の計画である。低層かつ高密度の都市居住における集合住宅の形式を模索することは我々の重要なテーマである。この計画で考えたのは、25〜40㎡の空間を単位とする住戸の集合の仕方である。変形敷地×3層分の仮想ボリュームの中に、ヴォイドを中心とし、その周りをソリッドな単位ボリュームが衛星のように取り巻く同心円状の構造を想定する。すると、単位空間、単位に囲まれた中心、単位空間同士の隙間、単位の集合の外部、と質の異なった4種類の空間が発生する。それにダイアグラムを合致させることで、個／共／公のそれぞれの空間については守られた或いは開かれた感覚を、またそれらの関係性については距離の感覚を調整することが可能になる。通りに沿った住戸ボリュームは、面として公共空間の輪郭をつくり、また通りと共用空間を隔て、住戸に囲われた共用空間の親密さのようなものを担保している。住戸ボリューム同士の隙間は共用空間から周囲が垣間見える場所であり、かつ共用空間と各住戸をつなぐ緩衝体となっている。隣地の空地と連担する残余空間は住戸空間を周囲に向かって開くための緩衝体となり、接地階においては住戸の専用庭となる。この集合のルールが単体の建築に留まらず、面的に広げて捉えた場合に有効な手法に発展し得るかどうかは次の課題となるだろう。
In this project, a three-story, 11-unit condominium is built in an area where low-rise residences, apartments, shops and temples are lining the street in the northern part of Kyoto City. For us, it is an important theme to grope for an ideal format of an apartment building in low-rise and

サンタアガータ
Sant' Agata
Sant' Agata Corp. / Shinichi Hayasaki + Kazuhiro Hirao / VIDZ Architects

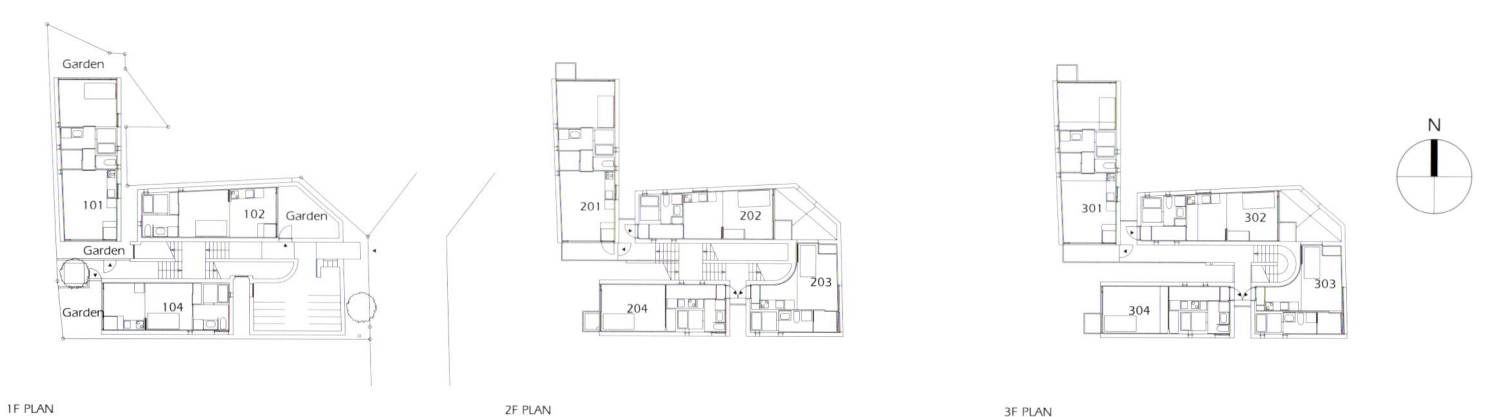

1F PLAN　　　　　2F PLAN　　　　　3F PLAN

Data

Title
Sant' Agata

Developer
Sant' Agata Corp.

Architect
Shinichi Hayasaki + Kazuhiro Hirao
VIDZ Architects

Location
Kamigyo-ku, Kyoto city

Site area
240.07m²

Building area
138.57m²

Total floor area
380.0m²

Area
26.89-39.14m²

Structure
RC

Completion
March, 2006

Materials
Exterior Wall :
　urethane painting on
　exposed concrete
　water- repellent coating on
　exposed concrete
Public Wall :
　urethane painting on
　exposed concrete

Materials
Public Floor :
　waterproofing mortal trowel finish
Interior Wall :
　vinyl cloth
Interior Floor :
　flooring, hard PVC

Photo
Yoshiharu Matsumura

high-density areas in cities. In this plan, we examine a method to integrate 25- to 40-square-meter units into a building. Within a volume of three floors on an irregular site, assume that you should build a concentric structure where a void is at the center and solid unitary volumes are around it as if they were moons. This consequently creates four types of spaces with different quality: unitary volumes, central void surrounded by the volumes, openings between the unitary volumes and the outside of the combinations of the units. By applying a diagram as appropriate, it becomes possible to give a sense of either security or openness to the private, common and public spaces individually and to adjust a feeling of distance between them in terms of their interrelationships. The residential volumes facing the street outlines the building as part of public space and, at the same time, separates the street and the common space, maintaining a sense of intimacy in the common space surrounded by the residential units. One can catch a glimpse of the outside from the common space through openings between the residential volumes; these openings also serve as buffers to connect between the common space and the individual units. The remaining space having a collective presence with the adjacent vacant land serves as a buffer to open the residential space toward the surroundings, and, for the units on the ground level, offers exclusive gardens. Our next challenge is to determine if this rule for collection can effectively be developed and applied to not only a single building but also to an extensive zone or area.

1
道路側外観の部分。奥に共用空間が見える
The exterior on the roadside revealing the common space at the back.

2
共用部3階廊下。ここから住棟間のすき間を通って各戸にアプローチする
Corridor of the common section on the third floor. Through the slit openings between units, one can approach individual units.

3
共用部階段見上げ。外壁によって切り取られた空を見る
When looked up from the stairs in the common section, one can see the sky cut out by the external walls.

4
102住戸：壁に囲まれた庭とつながった部屋
Unit #102: This room is connected to the garden surrounded by the walls.

5
304住戸：水廻り上部はスラブで仕切られた同じ面積分のロフトになっている
Unit #304: Above the kitchen and bathroom is a loft separated by the slab and having a same area as that of the wet area.

6
303住戸：部屋からキッチンを見る
Unit #303: The kitchen seen from the living room.

7
301住戸：それぞれ外部に面した2つの部屋は水廻りを通して連続している
Unit #301: The two rooms facing the outside are connected via the wet area.

DESIGNERS' APARTMENTS in JAPAN
Architect-Designed High-Rise CONDOMINIUMS

略歴
Biographies

アシハラヒロコ
Hiroko Ashihara
P-067

東京生まれ。日本女子大学住居学科卒業。アシハラヒロコデザイン事務所代表。個人邸では、建築設計、デザイン、コーディネーションに至るまでのトータリティーを、又、都心最高級マンションでは設計コンセプトにはじまり、外観・共用部・専有部・造園等まで幅広く建築デザインを手掛け、高い評価を得ている。主な作品として、リストランテ濱崎、京都室町・紫野和久傳、番町パークハウスなど。家具デザインの分野でも、独自の視点から作品を発表。イタリア家具会社から世界各国へ発売されイギリス等で人気を博している。

Born in Tokyo. Graduated from Department of Housing and Architecture, Japan Women's University. President of Ashihara Hiroko Design Office Co., Ltd. Has earned a high reputation for the totality of her architectural design, designing, and coordination in high-grade condominiums. Also has been given high marks for her design concept and various architectural designs ranging from exteriors to common areas, exclusively possessed areas, and landscapes. Her major works include Ristorante Hamasaki, Murasakino-Wakuden (Muromachi, Kyoto) and Bancho Parkhouse. Has introduced works designed with her unique point of view in the field of furniture designing. Her pieces have been sold all over the world through an Italian furniture company and have become popular in UK.

アースケイプ / 熊谷玄・団塚栄喜
Earthscape / Gen Kumagai · Eiki Danzuka
P-133

コンテンポラリーアートをバックボーンにランドスケープを作りつづけているデザイナーユニット。代表作は「晴海トリトンスクエア」「みなとみらいガーデンスクエア」「丸の内オアゾ」など。

Earthscape is a unit of landscape architects, which creates landscapes based on the context of contemporary art. Their works includes the Harumi Triton Square, Minato Mirai Garden Square and Marunouchi OAZO North Building.

アニエスベー
agnès b.
P-061

フランス・ヴェルサイユ生まれ。フランスのファッション誌「ELLE」でファッション・スタイリストを担当したことから彼女のモードに関わる人生が始まり、1975年にパリの中心、レ・アールのジュール通りに最初のブティックをオープン。以来、時代に左右されない新しい着こなしをさりげなく示し、世代・性別を問わず、世界中のさまざまな人々から支持され続けている。

Born in Versailles, France. Her life in the fashion world started when she became a fashion stylist of "Elle", a fashion magazine in France. Opened her first boutique on Rue du Jour in Halles at the center of Paris in 1975. Has casually presented new ways of dressing not influenced by trends ever since and has fascinated people all around the world regardless of age and gender.

安東孝一
Koichi Ando
P-009

アンドーギャラリー
1984年アンドーギャラリー設立。アート・建築・デザインのプロデュースを行う。「MODERN」(六耀社)、「NEW BLOOD」六耀社)、「くうかん」(ニューハウス出版)、「Graphic」(六耀社)、「インタビュー」(青幻舎)など、著書多数。「THE TOKYO TOWERS」では、片山正通氏がデザインする＜シータワー＞49・50階のラウンジ＆ゲストルーム、グエナエル・ニコラ氏がデザインする＜ミッドタワー＞54・55階のラウンジ＆ゲストルームをプロデュースする。

ANDO GALLERY
Established ANDO GALLERY in 1984. Engaged in production of art, architecture and design solutions. The author of various books including "MODERN: Art, Architecture and Design in Japan" (Rikuyosha Co., Ltd.), "NEW BLOOD: Art, Architecture and Design in Japan" (Rikuyosha Co., Ltd), "Kukan" (New HOUSE Publishing Co., Ltd.), "Graphic" (Rikuyosha Co., Ltd.) and "Interview" (Seigensha Art Publishing, Inc.). In "THE TOKYO TOWERS" project, he produced the lounge and guest rooms on the 49th and 50th floors of the SEA TOWER designed by Masamichi Katayama and the lounge and guest rooms on the 54th and

55th floors of the MID TOWER designed by Gwenael Nicolas.

石橋清志
Kiyoshi Ishibashi
P-169

建築家
株式会社石橋清志建築設計事務所　代表取締役
1948　大阪生まれ
1974　大阪工業大学　建築学科卒業
1974　今西建築デザインルーム入社
1982　商空間デザイン賞　佳作賞
　　　（日本店舗設計家協会）
1982　サインデザイン賞　入選
　　　（日本サインデザイン協会）
1985　石橋清志建築設計事務所　設立
1989　(株) 石橋清志建築設計事務所　設立
2003　大阪都市景観建築賞
　　　大阪府知事賞　受賞
2004　あたたかな住空間デザインコンペ
　　　特別賞

Architect
Ishibashi Kiyoshi Architect design office inc. president
1948 : Born in Osaka
1974 : Graduated from Institute of Technology Architect major
1974 : Employed by Imanishi design Room Company
1982 : Shokukan Design Award honorable Mention (Nihon Tenpo Design Association)/Sign Design Award winner (Nihon Sign Design Association)
1985 : Open Ishibashi Kiyoshi Architectural design office
1989 : Established the Ishibashi Kiyoshi Architectural design office inc.
2003 : Awarded Osaka city landscape award (Osaka prefecture governor award)
2005: Special Award, The 8th Warm Living Space Design Competition

伊藤圭太
Keita Ito
P-009

株式会社 山下設計
1970年静岡県出身。晴海トリトンスクエアの施設（建物）の設計及びランドスケープデザインを担当。リカルド・ボフィル（バルセロナ）と協働で川崎西口開発商業施設ラゾーナの設計を手掛けた。「THE TOKYO TOWERS」ではソラ・アソシエイツの藤田氏と共にランドスケープデザインを担当する。

Yamashita Sekkei Inc.
Born in Shizuoka in 1970. Planned and designed the Harumi Toriton Square facilities (buildings) and its landscape. Co-worked with Mr. Richard Bofill (Barcelona) while designing Lazona Kawasaki, the commercial facilities developed on the western side of the JR Kawasaki station. He also partnered with Mr. Hisakazu Fujita (sola associates) to design landscapes in the "THE TOKYO TOWERS" project.

上田智晴
Tomoharu Ueda
P-184

(有) 上田智晴アーキテクツ
1988年　大阪芸術大学芸術学部建築学科卒業
1988年　(株) ヘキサ入社、住宅・集合住宅・オフィスビル等の建築デザインに従事
1992年　H/Pデザイン (株) 入社、店舗等商業施設のデザインに従事
1992年　THX 一級建築士事務所設立
1993年　事務所運営をパートナーシップ体制とする
1997年　ヨーロッパ〜中近東〜北アフリカを巡る建築行脚の旅に出る
1998年　帰国
2002年　(有) 上田智晴アーキテクツ設立〜現在に至る

Ueda Tomoharu Architects inc.
1988 Graduated from Architecture Department, Faculty of Fine Arts,
Osaka University of Arts
1988 Joined Hexa. Responsible for architectural designs of private homes, housing complexes and office buildings
1992 Joined H/P Design. Involved in designing commercial facilities including outlets
1992 Established THX first-class architect office
1993 Reorganized THX first-class architect office to a partnership
1997 Traveled through Europe, Middle East and North Africa to see different styles of architecture
1998 Returned to Japan
2002 Established Ueda Tomoharu Architects and continues his activities

内原智史
Satoshi Uchihara
P-039

内原智史デザイン事務所代表
主なプロジェクトに、六本木ヒルズ アリーナ、愛宕グリーンヒルズ景観照明計画、東京国際空港第2ターミナル羽田。1994年より、平等院、金閣寺、銀閣寺などのライティングデザインを手掛ける。

Representative, Uchihara Creative Lighting Design Inc.
His main projects include Roppongi Hills Arena, the landscape lighting project of Atago Green Hills, Passenger Terminal 2 at the Tokyo International Airport (Haneda). Has been involved in landscape lighting of Japanese historic temples such as Byodoin Temple, Kinkakuji Temple, and Ginkakuji Temple since 1994.

太田道夫
Michio Ohta
P-187

一級建築士事務所キメラ
1953年　滋賀県生まれ
1971年　大阪市立都島工業高等学校　建築科卒業
1986年　太田道夫建築設計事務所設立
1999年　一級建築士事務所キメラ設立
おもに個人住宅・集合住宅・福祉施設・商業ビルなどの建築を手掛ける

CHIMERA ARCHITECTS
1953 Born in Shiga
1971 Graduated from Architecture Studies at Miyakojima Technical High School in Osaka
1986 Established Michio Ohta Architectural Design Office
1999 Established CHIMERA ARCHITECTS
Mainly works on designing detached houses, apartments and condominiums, welfare facilities and commercial buildings.

大平直子
Naoko Ohira
P-035

鹿島建設　関西支店　建築設計部
1970年兵庫県生まれ
1994年大阪市立大学生活科学部住居学科卒業
大阪府建築士会会員
日本建築士会連合会　専攻建築士
第52回青年技術者 (設計部門)、兵庫県人間サイズの街づくり賞などを受賞
関西を中心に、住宅、オフィス、ホテル、物販店舗等多岐に渡る設計を手掛ける。

Architectural Design Department, Kajima Corporation
Born in Hyogo Prefecture in 1970
Graduated from Housing and Environmental Design Course, Faculty of Human Life Science, Osaka City University
Member, Osaka Association of Architects & Building Engineers
Specialist architect, Japan Federation of Architects & Building Engineers Associations
Has won the 52nd AJJ Young Architects Award (Design), Hyogo Human-sized Town Development Award, etc.
She has been engaged in a wide range of architectural designs including private residences, offices, hotels and shops.

片山正通
Masamichi Katayama
P-009

ワンダーウォール
1966年岡山県生まれ。2000年ワンダーウォール設立。ブティックやショールーム、レストランなどのショップデザインの他、プロダクトや家具、照明などの活動の場は多岐に渡る。明確なコンセプトのもとに展開される斬新なデザインが、国内はもとより海外でも高い評価を得ている。

Wonderwall Inc.
Born in Okayama in 1966. Established Wonderwall Inc. in 2000. His comprehensive design activities cover not only shop interiors of boutiques, showrooms, and restaurants but also furniture, lighting and other products. His novel designs with clearly defined concepts are rated very high both in Japan and overseas.

金田篤士
Atsushi Kaneda
P-133

ワークテクト
国際的なネットワークと豊富な海外経験を生かし、ホテル&リゾート、商業施設、娯楽施設などの照明デザインを提案。代表作は「パンパシフィックホテル横浜」「フォレストヒルズゴルフ&リゾート」など。

Worktecht Corporation
Through his international network and vast overseas experience, he delivers his

own style of lighting design, working on projects such as resort hotels as well as commercial and entertainment facilities. His major works include Pan Pacific Hotel Yokohama and Forest Hills Golf & Resort.

小菊健司
Kenji Kogiku
P-039
（株）フリークス設計事務所代表
一級建築士。主なプロジェクトに、ニセコ東急ゴルフクラブ、武蔵工業大学環境情報部横浜キャンパス、渋谷マークシティ（プロジェクトリーダー）等その他多数。
Representative, Freecs Co., Ltd.
Registered architect of the first class. His main projects include Niseko Tokyu Golf Club, the Yokohama campus of Engineering, Environmental and Information studies of Musashi Institute of Technology, and SHIBUYA MARK CITY (as a project leader.)

酒匂克之
Katsuyuki Sakoh
P-009
丘の上事務所
東京造形大学造形学部デザイン学科卒業、近藤康夫デザイン事務所に勤務。2001年丘の上事務所を設立。丘の上のように人を身近に感じられるスタンスで、レストランやショップ、住宅、プロダクトなど様々なデザイン活動を展開。
OKANOUE
Graduated from the Department of Design, Faculty of Zokei (creating art and design), Tokyo Zokei University and joined Yasuo Kondo Design. Established his own office named OKANOUE in 2001. This name meaning "on the hill" in Japanese represents his attitude toward architectural design where he familiarize himself with people and their residences as if viewing from the hill, and he designs restaurants, shops, houses, and other products based on this approach.

崎 丈晴
Takeharu Saki
P-009
オフィス・サキ
1999年オフィス・サキ設立。個人邸、マンションのパブリックエリア、モデルルーム等の居住空間から、リゾートホテル、企業ショールーム、展示会等のコマーシャルデザインまでを手がける。家具やアートワーク、小物までを含めた、トータルでの提案も行っている。
Office SAKI
Established Office SAKI in 1999. He engages in residential spatial planning for private houses, public area for condominiums, and model rooms, as well as commercial designing for resort-hotels, corporate showrooms and exhibitions. He also pays great attention to furniture, art works and knick-knacks that work well together as a whole.

島田佳代子
Kayoko Shimada
P-009
アイランド・アルファ
2001年アイランド・アルファ設立。集合住宅、個人住宅のインテリアコーディネートの他、建材メーカーの商品開発やインテリア・アクセサリーの企画等にも従事。社団法人インテリア産業協会主催「インテリアコーディネーションコンテスト'93」では通産大臣賞を受賞。
Island alpha
Established Island alpha in 2001. She involves not only in interior coordination of housing complexes and private houses but also product development of architectural materials and interior accessory planning. She was awarded the Minister of International Trade and Industry Prize in Interior Coordination Contest 1993 sponsored by Japan Interior Industry Association.

東海林弘靖
Hiroyasu Shouji
P-133
ライトデザイン
自然の美しい光との出会いの感動を糧に、超高層建築のファサードから美術館、飲食空間まで幅広い光のデザインを行っている。代表作は「まつもと市民芸術館」「MIKIMOTO GINZA2」など。
LIGHTDESIGN INC.
In attempts to bring a captivating feeling of being enveloped by beautiful natural light, he designs a wide range of lighting facilities for such spaces as facades of skyscrapers, museums and dining spaces. His representative works include Matsumoto Performing Arts Centre and MIKIMOTO GINZA2.

菅匡史
Tadashi Suga
P-160, 177, 181, 190
建築家
1966年兵庫県生まれ
1989年近畿大学理工学部建築学科卒業
1993年菅匡史建築研究所を設立
2004年American Wood Design Award 受賞
日本建築士会連合会賞受賞
神戸市景観ポイント賞受賞
Born in Hyogo prefecture in 1966. After graduating the Department of Architecture, School of Science and Engineering, Kinki University, he established Suga Architects Office Co., Ltd in 1993.
Awards:
2004 American Wood Design Award
Japan Federation of Architects & Building Engineers Associations Award
Kobe City Landscape Point Award

高取邦和
Kunikazu Takatori
P-089
株式会社 高取空間計画
東京芸術大学美術学部工芸科卒業
1970年ポテトデザイン研究室（のちの「スーパーポテト」）を共同設立
1988年（有）高取邦和設計室設立
1996年（株）高取空間計画設立。多摩美術大学非常勤講師。
＜主な作品＞
「バーラジオ」('73)、「イッセイ・ミヤケ」('90)、「富山県こども未来館インテリア」('92)、「松栄寿司」('93)、「4°C」('93～)、「茨城県自然博物館インテリア」('95)、「CKカルバン・クライン」('95～)、「レストラン・ルッツォーロ&ウーム」('98)、住宅：「軽井沢A氏邸」、「柿の木坂A氏邸」、「那須T氏邸」等
TAKATORI KUUKAN KEIKAKU
Graduated from Craft Course, Faculty of Fine Arts at Tokyo National University of Fine Arts and Music. Jointly established Potato Design Laboratory (later to be renamed as SUPER POTATO CO., LTD.)in 1970. Established Kunikazu Takatori Design Studio in 1988 and TAKATORI KUUKAN KEIKAKU in 1996. He is also a part-time lecturer at Tama Art University.
<Major works>
Bar Radio('73); ISSEY MIYAKE ('90); Interior planning for TOYAMA CHILDREN'S CENTER ('92); susi matsue ('93); 4 Degrees Centigrade ('93-); Interior planning for IBARAKI NATURE MUSEUM ('95); ck Calvin Klein ('95-); Restaurant L'uzzolo & BAR ym ('98); Private houses: Mr. A's residence in Karuizawa; Mr. A's residence in Kakinokizaka; Mr. T's residence in Nasu; etc

田辺久人
Hisato Tanabe
P-067, 109
三菱地所設計 住環境設計部 統括部長
これまで日本の建築界に多くの実績を残してきた三菱地所設計の住環境設計部。その統括部長として、デザイナー&エンジニアの俊英を率いて活躍している。豊かな経験と感性に裏打ちされた数々の業績は、国内外で高い評価を受けている。作品としては「TOKYO TWIN PARKS」「THE HOUSE Minami-Azabu」「コットンハーバータワーズ」等多数。
Manager, Living Environment Design & Engineering Department, Mitsubishi Jisho Sekkei, Inc.
Living Environment Design & Engineering Department has long achieved many accomplishments in the architectural industry in Japan. Tanabe has been active as manager of the department and led groups of the best and brightest designers and engineers. His accomplishments based on profound experience as well as sensibility have highly been appreciated both domestically and internationally.
His works include Tokyo Twin Parks, The House Minami-Azabu, and Cotton Harbor Towers.

塚田豊男
Toyoo Tsukada
P-057
鹿島建設株式会社 関西支店建築設計部
1992年 京都大学工学部建築学科 修士課程終了
鹿島建設株式会社
設計・エンジニアリング事業本部入社
1998年 同社 関西支店建築設計部
2001年 グッドデザイン賞
　「世界救世教　神戸教会」
2002年 建築協会
　第49回　青年技術者選出
2003年 大阪市将来構想委員（～2005年）

2004年 大阪まちなみ賞
「中央復建コンサルタンツ本社ビル」
その他、個人住宅から超高層オフィス、研究施設など手がける
Architectural Design Department, Kansai Branch, Kajima Corporation
1992 Graduated from Department of Architecture and Architectural Engineering, Graduate School of Engineering, Kyoto University; Joined the Design and Engineering Division, Kajima Corporation
1998 Architectural Design Department, Kansai Branch, Kajima Corporation
2001 Awarded Good Design Award (Kobe Church, MOA)
2002 Selected as one of the prospective young architects at the 49th AAJ Award
2003 Appointed a member of the Future Planning Committee, Osaka City (-2005)
2004 Awarded Osaka Landscape Award (Chuo Fukken Consultants Head Office)
He has also actively designed a wide range of buildings from personal residences to high-rise office building and R&D facilities.

テュラン・デューダ
Turan Duda
P-079
デューダ&ペイン建築設計事務所
シーザーペリ&アソシエーツ建築設計事務所の主幹デザイナーとして、高層ビルはじめ、様々な設計を通じてその名を世界に知らしめる。1997年、ジェフェリー・ペイン氏と共にデューダ&ペイン建築設計事務所を設立。主な作品(シーザーペリ&アソシエーツ)に、ニューマディソンスクエアガーデン(米国・ニューヨーク州)など。光井純氏とのコラボレーション作品として「国立国際美術館(大阪)」「倉吉パークスクエア」などがある。
Duda/Paine Architects, LLP
Developed a high reputation for producing various designs, particularly those of skyscrapers, as the chief designer of Pelli Clarke Pelli Architects. Established Duda/Paine Architects, LLP with his partner, Mr. Jeffrey Paine, in 1997. His major works include the new Madison Square Garden (New York, US) by Pelli Clarke Pelli Architects, and National Museum of Art (Osaka) and Kurayoshi Park Square both in collaboration with Mr. Jun Mitsui.

友澤薫
Kaoru Tomosawa
P-009
株式会社日建スペースデザイン
1967年東京都出身。インテリアデザイナー。ホテルや店舗、住宅、オフィス、テーマパーク、プロダクト等、多岐にわたって活動。携わったプロジェクトは、全日空オアシスタワー、丸の内オアゾ、他多数。「THE TOKYO TOWERS」では、エントランスホール、ラウンジ等、共用スペースのインテリアデザインを担当。
NIKKEN SPACE DESIGN Ltd.
Born in Tokyo in 1967. Interior designer. Active in various fields including hotels, shops, houses, offices, theme parks and products. The main projects are ANA HOTEL OITA OASISTOWER, Marunouchi oazo, etc. Responsible for the interior design of the common space like entrance halls and lounges in THE TOKYO TOWERS project.

南部昌亮
Masaaki Nambu
P-049, 115
フォワードスタイル株式会社代表
アメリカ建築設計事務所ONUMA & WOOD ASSOCIATES, INC.、アルフレックス・ジャパンを経て、2003年「フォワードスタイル株式会社」設立。都心のレジデンシャルスペース、エグゼクティブオフィスを中心に設計・デザイン、施工監修までをトータルに行う。時代を読み解く独自の感性ととともに、空間のトーナリティを創造するスタイルと多彩な実績に基づくノウハウで、五感に触れる上質な空間デザインを発信。
Representative of FORWARD STYLE Co., Ltd.
After working for an American architect studio, ONUMA & WOOD ASSOCIATES, INC. and ARFLEX JAPAN LTD., established "FORWARD STYLE Co., Ltd." in 2003. Engaged in overall coordination of planning and designing including the supervision of construction, mainly for residential-space and executive offices. Taking advantage of his unique sensitivity to interpret the times, his style to create the tonality of space and the know-how based on his achievements in a wide range of activities, he delivers high quality spatial designs that flatter the senses.

グエナエル・ニコラ
Gwenael Nicolas
P-009
キュリオシティ
1966年フランス生まれ。1991年RCA修了後来日。1998年デザインスタジオ「キュリオシティ」設立。デザインが人にどのような時間を提示できるのか、をテーマに実用的で美しいデザインを提案し続ける。スペース、プロダクト、グラフィックに至るまで幅広い分野で活動中。
CURIOCITY Inc.
Born in France in 1966. Graduated from Royal College of Art (RCA) and came to Japan in 1991. Established CURIOSITY Inc., a design studio, in 1998. Has been introducing practical and beautiful designs focusing on his theme: How design affects the way people spend their time. Actively engaged in wide-ranging fields from designing spaces and products to graphics.

野村宏幸
Hiroyuki Nomura
P-009
株式会社ワークテクト
1971年福井県出身。照明デザイナー。ホテル等の商業施設や公共施設などの景観照明やインテリア照明のデザインを手掛ける。台湾宣簡県政資料館、メリルリンチジャパン、ザ・ビーチタワー沖縄等。「THE TOKYO TOWERS」では、エントランスホール、ラウンジの照明デザインを担当。
Worktecht Corporation
Born in Fukui in 1971. Lighting designer. Worked on landscape lighting and interior lighting designs for various commercial and public facilities including hotels including Yilan County Historical Museum in Taiwan; Merrill Lynch Japan Securities Co., Ltd.; and The Beach Tower Okinawa (hotel). In "THE TOKYO TOWERS" project, he is responsible for lighting design of the entrance halls and the lounges of the high-rise condominium buildings.

橋本夕紀夫
Yukio Hashimoto
P-025
橋本夕紀夫デザインスタジオ
デザイナー・女子美術大学短大非常勤講師・愛知県立芸術大学非常勤講師
1986年、株式会社スーパーポテト入社。
1996年、橋本夕紀夫デザインスタジオ設立。
1997年、ナショップライティングコンテスト優秀賞受賞。
1998年、ナショップライティングアワード・ナショップ賞受賞、JCD奨励賞受賞。
1999年、JCD奨励賞受賞。
2000年、JCD優秀賞受賞。
hashimoto yukio design studio Co.,Ltd.
Designer/Part-time lecturer at Junior College of Art and Design, Joshibi University of Art and Design/Part-time lecturer at Aichi Prefectural University of Fine Arts and Music
1986 Joined Super Potato Co., Ltd.
1996 Established hashimoto yukio design studio Co.,Ltd.
1997 2nd Prize, Nashop Lighting Award
1998 Nashop Award of Nashop Lighting Award; Encouragement Award of JCD Design Award
1999 Encouragement Award of JCD Design Award
2000 2nd Prize Award of JCD Design Award

蓮見由実
Yumi Hasumi
P-089
株式会社メック・デザイン・インターナショナル
青山学院大学卒業。国際線客室乗務員として世界各地を訪れ、海外の建築・インテリアに影響を受け、後にインテリアデザイン事務所、ハウスメーカーの経験を経て、(株)メック・デザイン・インターナショナルに在籍。インテリアクリエイティブワークに携わる。
<主な作品>
「Wコンフォートタワーズ」、「パークハウス外苑西」等
Mec design International Corporation
Graduated from Aoyama Gakuin University. As a cabin attendant on international flights, she visited various parts of the world and was influenced by overseas architecture and interior. After working for an interior design office and a housing maker, she joined Mec design international Corporation. She is engaged in interior designing for creative works.
[Major works]
W Comfort Towers, Park House Gaien-Nishi, etc.

フェルナンド・バスケス
FernandoVazquez
P-049
1995年
フェルナンド・バスケス・スタジオ設立。1997年、エルビ・ベケット社を経て、2000年HNTB社のデザインディレクターに就任。
2002年KFXデザインを設立。
複合商業施設やエンターテイメント施設のマスタープランなど幅広い分野のデザインを手掛ける。アメリカ、日本、ヨーロッパ、東南アジア等の数多くのプロジェクトで活躍している。
Established FERNANDO VAZQUEZ/STUDIO in 1995. Joined ELLERBE BECKET in 1997 and became the design director at HNTB in 2000. Established KFX design in 2002. Has been involved in a wide variety of designing activities including master plans of commercial complexes and amusement facilities. Active in many projects in the US, Japan, Europe, and Southeast Asia.

塙 哲夫
Tetsuo Hanawa
P-039
(有)塙ランドスケープデザイン代表。
主なプロジェクトに、FIVE STAR、幕張ベイタウンブエナテラーサ、東京ツインパークス他。多数の造園設計を手掛ける。
Representative, HANAWA LANDSACAPE DESIGN
His main projects include FIVE STAR, Makuhari Baytown Buena Terraza, Tokyo Twin Parks, etc. Has engaged in designs of many landscape architectures.

浜田雅子
Masako Hamada
P-009
浜田デザインワークス
女子美術大学卒業。ホテル、クラブハウス、住宅等のデザイン業務に従事後、1992年浜田デザインワークスを設立。主に集合住宅の部材開発、顧客フリープラン対応、インテリアデザイン。総合プロデュース業務に携わる。あらゆる視点から多面的に暮らしを捉えたインテリアデザインの構築は、多くの人の評価を集めている。「THE TOKYO TOWERS」では、モデルルームデザインのプロデュースだけでなく、販売住戸の内装デザインも担当。
Hamada Design Works
Graduated from Joshibi University of Art and Design. After being engaged in such business design projects as hotels, clubhouses and housings, she established the Hamada Design Works, where she is mainly engaged in development of structural members for apartment houses, customized house planning, interior design and general housing planning activities. Her interior design is highly evaluated for creating interior designs based on the perception of lifestyles from various viewpoints. In "THE TOKYO TOWERS" project, she designed the interiors of not only model rooms but also units for sale.

浜野安宏
Yasuhiro Hamano
P-163
ライフスタイル・プロデューサー
株式会社 浜野総合研究所 代表取締役社長
ハマノコンセプト株式会社 代表取締役
多摩美術大学 客員教授
特定非営利活動法人
　渋谷・青山景観整備機構 専務理事
キュー・アックス株式会社 顧問
特定非営利活動法人
　スクールデザインネット 理事
社団法人 太平洋諸島地域研究所 常務理事
Life style producer
President and Chief Executive Officer, Hamano Institute Inc.
President and Chief Executive Officer, Hamano Concept Inc.
Visiting professor, Tama Art University
Managing director, Shibuya Aoyama Landscape Formation Organization, N. P. O.
Advisor, Q-AX Co., Ltd.
Board member, School Design Net
Managing director, Japan Institute for Pacific Studies (JAIPAS)

早崎伸一
Shinichi Hayasaki
P-197
1966年長崎県生まれ
1989年京都大学建築学科卒業
1989年〜1994年長谷工コーポレーション
1997年以降造形工房
　(現VIDZ建築設計事務所)パートナー
1966 Born in Nagasaki
1989 Graduated from School of Architecture, Faculty of Engineering, Kyoto University
1989 Joined HASEKO Corporation (-1994)
A partner in Zokei Kobo (the current VIDZ Architects) since 1997

平尾和洋
Kazuhiro Hirao
P-197
1966年大阪府生まれ
1989年京都大学建築学科卒業、パリ建築大学ラビレット校、京都大学助手
1997年以降造形工房(現VIDZ建築設計事務所)パートナー
現在、立命館大学助教授
1966 Born in Osaka
1989 Graduated from the School of Architecture, Faculty Engineering, Kyoto University
1992 Trainee at Ecole Nationale Superieure d'Architecture de Paris La Villette and Assistant lecturer at Kyoto University(-1998)
A partner in Zoukei Kobo (the current VIDZ Architects) since 1997
Associate Professor of Ritsumeikan University at present

藤田久数
Hisakazu Fujita
P-009
ソラ・アソシエイツ
1957年愛知県出身。
ランドスケープデザイナーおよびライティングデザイナーとして国内外で広く活動。携わったプロジェクトは、晴海トリトンスクエア、愛知万博グローバルコモン4、他多数。「THE TOKYO TOWERS」では、山下設計の伊藤氏と共にランドスケープおよびライティングデザインを担当。
sola associates
Born in Aichi in 1957.
Active as a landscape designer as well as lighting designer both at home and abroad. His main projects include Harumi Triton Square and Global Common 4 of EXPO 2005 Aichi, Japan. In THE TOKYO TOWERS project he is responsible for landscape and lighting designs with Mr.Ito from Yamashita Sekkei Inc.

船越康弘
Yasuhiro Funakoshi
P-009
株式会社 山下設計
1955年兵庫県生まれ。晴海トリトンスクエア、アクアドームくまもとなど多数のプロジェクトで、建築デザイン監修・プロジェクトマネージャーを務める。「THE TOKYO TOWERS」ではツインタワーのファサードを含むランドスケープデザインを監修。
Yamashita Sekkei Inc.
Born in Hyogo in 1955. Has supervised architecture design and managed many projects including Harumi Triton Square and Aqua Dome Kumamoto. He supervised the landscape designing of "The Tokyo Towers" project including the facade of the twin towers.

別府ひとみ
Hitomi Beppu
P-039, 143
スタジオ・ボングスト
町田ひろ子インテリアアカデミー第4回グランプリコンクールにて大賞受賞、最優秀賞受賞。フリーのコーディネーターとして独立した後、「スタジオ・ボングスト」を設立。主に戸建て、集合住宅デザイン、グリーンコーディネート、照明コーディネート等のトータルスペースデザインを手掛ける。
Studio Boun Gusto Co., Ltd.
Won the grand prize and the first prize in the 4th Grand Prix Contest organized by Hiroko Machida Interior Co-ordinator Academy. After working as a coordinator on freelance basis, she established "Studio Boun Gusto Co., Ltd". Mainly devoted in overall spatial design including designs for residence and housing complex, horticultural coordination and lighting coordination.

マイケル・ベドナー
Michael J. Bedner
P-133
HBAはホテルデザインを主とするホスピタリティ・デザインの先駆的企業。
「リッツ・カールトン」「マンダリン・オリエンタル」など世界各地の名だたるホテルの空間デザインを数多く手掛ける。
HBA (Hirsh Bedner Associates)
HBA is a pioneering company focusing on the hospitality design mainly for hotels and has been engaged in various architec

堀江徹
Toru Horie
P-009
株式会社ワークテクト
1963年北海道出身。
エンジニアリングデザイナー。ホテルや劇場、商業空間の照明デザインの他、音響や映像等、演出も手掛ける。CHANEL GINZA、六本木ヒルズなど参加したプロジェクトは多数。「THE TOKYO TOWERS」では、エントランスホール、ラウンジの照明デザインを担当。

Worktecht Corporation
Born in Hokkaido in 1963.
Engineering designer. Designed lighting for hotels, theaters and other commercial facilities and spaces as well as audio/visual productions. Engaged in CHANEL GINZA, Roppongi Hills and many other projects. In "THE TOKYO TOWERS" project, he designed lighting for the entrance halls and the lounges.

光井純
Jun Mitsui
P-025, 039, 079, 133
建築家
光井純アンドアソシエーツ建築設計事務所（株）、シーザーペリアンドアソシエーツジャパン（株）代表。主なプロジェクトに、羽田空港第2ターミナル、NTT新宿本社ビル、愛宕グリーンヒルズ他。コンベンションホテル、オフィスビル、都市開発など多彩な活動を展開し、グッドデザイン賞など受賞多数。また日米両国において建築士資格を有し、米国建築家協会の会員及び日本建築家協会の会員としても活動を行い、協働的創造とデザインオンレスポンスの理念のもとに、敷地の持つポテンシャルを最大限引き出しながら付加価値の高い都市空間と建築を数多く生み出している。

Architect
Representative director of Jun Mitsui & Associates Inc. Architects and Cesar Pelli & Associates, Inc. His major projects include Passenger Terminal 2 of the Tokyo International Airport (Haneda), NTT Shinjuku Headquarters Bldg. and Atago Green Hills. Actively working in designs of convention hotels, office buildings and many other architectural designs as well as urban development, he has won Good Design Award and other awards. He is a licensed architect in both Japan and the USA and has been acting as a member of American Institute of Architects (AIA) and Japan Institute of Architects (JIA). With the concept of "collaborative process" (creation with a client-oriented approach, which aims to offer the maximum value added to a client's investment in the form of design) and "design on response" (a design approach to see architecture as an aspect of culture and a living creature which forms a part of the townscape and develops with the town), he has fully brought out the potential of each site and created a number of high value-added urban spaces and buildings.

谷内田章夫
Akio Yachida
P-193
1975年 横浜国立大学建築学科卒業。
1978年 東京大学大学院建築専門修士修了。同年、北山恒、木下道郎とワークショップ設立。
1995年 谷内田章夫／ワークショップ設立。

Graduated from the Architecture Department, Yokohama National University in 1975 and obtained his master degree of architecture at the Graduate School of Engineering, The University of Tokyo in 1978. In the same year, established a workshop with Koh Kitayama and Michio Kinoshita. Established AKIO YACHIDA / WORKSHOP in 1995.

柳田俊明
Toshiaki Yanagida
P-079
株式会社グリーンアンドアーツ（オリエンタルランドグループ）
住空間事業部長
リゾートをはじめ、複合型商業施設、ホテルなど、様々な事業で培われた造園・植栽技術を結集。オリエンタルランドグループの一員として、夢と感動を与える緑豊かなランドスケープを創造。
主な実績（造園・植栽事業）：「イクスピアリ」植栽工事監理・壁面緑化工事、「恵比寿ガーデンプレイス」新商業施設植栽工事など。

GREEN AND ARTS Co., LTD. (OLC Group)
Living Space Division Manager
GREEN AND ARTS Co., LTD combines technologies of landscape gardening and planting acquired through resorts, commercial complexes, hotels and other business operations to create green landscapes with dreams and impressions as a member of Oriental Land Group
Representative Works (landscaping and planting):
Supervision of planting and greening of walls at "Ikspiari" at Tokyo Disney Resort
Landscape gardening construction works for a new commercial district of "Yebisu Garden Place" and others

エリック・ロイド・ライト
Eric Lloyd Wright
P-151
アメリカで最も偉大な建築家と評される祖父フランク・ロイド・ライトの哲学、そして思想を受け継ぐライト家直系、唯一の建築家。フランク・ロイド・ライトが晩年に開いた建築学校「タリアセン・フェローシップ」で建築の全てを学び74才になる今も現役として、多くの建築デザインを手掛けている。今回、「M.M.MID SQUARE」では、みなとみらいという舞台からインスピレーションを得て巨匠フランク・ロイド・ライトの世界観を具現化する、新たな都市居住とみらいへ伝えたい日常を築き上げる。

He is the only architect who is a direct descendant of the Wright family. His grandfather, Frank Lloyd Wright is famous as the greatest architect in the U.S., and his philosophy and concept are taken over by his grand son, Eric. He learned all about architecture at the architecture school, the Taliesin Fellowship that had been opened by Frank Lloyd Wright in late life. Eric Lloyd Wright still works on many architecture designs at the age of 74. In the "M.M. MID SQUARE" project, he has designed new urban residences and lifestyles leading to the future to embody Frank Lloyd Wright's world-view, inspired by the arena of Minato Mirai.

若林広幸
Hiroyuki Wakabayashi
P-173
建築家（株）若林広幸建築研究所代表取締役
1949年 京都市生まれ
1967年（株）たち吉入社
同年（株）たち吉のホームエージェンシーである京都デザイン（株）に編入社
商品開発、企画デザイナーとして活躍
1972年 独立、インテリア設計事務所を自営しつつ我流で建築を学ぶ
1982年 若林広幸建築研究所設立
1994年 南海空港特急「rapi:t」をデザインし話題となる
主な受賞
1984年 SDレビュー入選
1988年 商環境デザイン大賞
　　　　SDレビュー入選
1991年 第9回京都府文化奨励賞
　　　　日本文化フォーラム・日本文化デザイン賞
1995年 「南海空港特急rapi:t」にブルーリボン賞
1996年 京阪宇治駅にグッドデザイン賞
2002年 「PIER 624」に大阪市ハウジングデザイン賞
2003年 「PIER624」にグッドデザイン賞
2004年 「北大路まちなか住宅コラボレーション02'」にグッドデザイン賞

Architect, representative director Studio Arch Hiroyuki Wakabayashi
1949 Born in Kyoto City, 1967 Transferred to Launched the Modern Tableware company called "ADAM & EVE" a home agency of Tachikichi Co.,Ltd. Joined Tachikichi Co.,Ltd. 1972 Became independent; self-taught architecture while running an interior design office. 1982 Established Studio Arch Hiroyuki Wakabayashi
1994 Designed rapi:t, airport special express, Nankai Electric Railway
Awards:
1984 Winner, SD Review
1988 Commercial Environmental Design Grand Prix
 Winner, SD Review
1991 Encouragement Prize, 9th Kyoto Culture Award
 Japan Culture Design Award, Japan Culture Forum
1995 Blue Ribbon Award for rapi:t, airport special express, Nankai Electric Railway
1996 Good Design Award for Uji Station, Uji Line, Keihan Traffic
2002 Osaka City Housing Design Award for Pier 624
2003 Good Design Award for Pier 624
2004 Good Design Award for "Kitaoji Machinaka Housing Collaboration 02'"

DESIGNERS' APARTMENTS in JAPAN
Architect-Designed
High-Rise CONDOMINIUMS

あとがき
Afterword

清水文夫
Fumio Shimizu

近年、東京・大阪・横浜などの大都市で、大規模な地域の再開発計画が数多く行われています。都市の居住環境の向上ならびに都市機能の高度化を図ることを目的とした都市計画で、地区内に業務・商業施設などを中心とした賑わいの場や周辺の環境との調和が図られた良好な居住環境が造られています。

その中に建つ高層タワー・マンションも周辺環境と調和を保ちながら、街のランドマークとなっています。都心ならではの利便性や眺望だけではなく、敷地内に充実したパブリック・スペースを設け、水と光と緑にあふれる環境を作り出しています。高層タワー・マンションにおけるこのような景観や都市環境は、そこに住む人に良質な生活文化を提供しています。

本書では、このような住まう歓びを存分に感じることのできる居住性を実

In recent years, many large-scale redevelopment projects have been undertaken in big cities including Tokyo, Osaka and Yokohama. In these city planning programs intended to improve urban living environments and sophisticate urban functions, excellent residential environments have been established, provided with business and commercial facilities and other gathering places on site while perfectly harmonized with surrounding environments.

Each high-rise tower condominium built in the project site serves as a landmark of the city while maintaining harmony with the local environment. Enjoying convenience and views unique to the city center, the towers also offer complete on-site public spaces and create an environment rich in light, water and green. Such landscaping and urban environments of high-rise tower condominiums provide residents with high-grade living culture.

現する計画とデザイン、開発の例を数多く収録しています。具体的な例では、足元から圧倒的な海が広がる恵まれたロケーションで、都心でありながらオーシャンフロントのリゾート気分が満喫できる環境。豊かな自然に彩られた四季折々の季節感が感じられるランドスケープ・デザインや、土地柄や街並みに溶け込む住居環境。医療機関や保育施設、ショッピング施設など、生活に必要な機能のほとんどを整えた充実した環境。住宅を中心とした街づくりで、広場や遊歩道などのオープンスペースを圧倒的な面積で占めたゆとりと潤いのある環境。また、様々なメニューでホテルライクに日常をもてなすコンシェルジュ・サービスやカフェラウンジやリラクゼーションルームなどの充実したパブリック・スペースを持った環境。など、単なる建物のデザインという開発だけでは満足出来なくなった住み手に対して、デベロッパーは都市を取り込んだ住環境の整備や取り組みなど、様々な提案をしています。

大都市の至る場所で計画されている、これからの都心生活を牽引するモデルタウン。そこには土地が育んできた伝統や文化を継承し、さらに徹底して住みやすさにこだわった新しい住宅地として、調和のとれた美しい都市風景がうまれつつあります。

今回も出版にあたり多くの方々にお世話になりました。根気よく最後まで担当して下さったグラフィック社の大田悟さん、翻訳者の宮坂聖一さんには本当にお世話になりました。また、美しい写真を提供して下さった著名な写真家の皆様、松村芳治氏にも心より感謝申し上げます。そして、膨大な資料を美しくレイアウトして下さった丹治竜一さん、本当に有り難うございました。

This book covers many examples of plans, designs and development projects realizing amenities enabling one to fully enjoy comfortable residential life. To be concrete, this book exemplifies a favorable environment where the sea expands right in front of the site, enabling one to enjoy a feeling as if one were staying at a ocean front resort hotel; a landscape design rich in nature, giving a sense of four seasons; a residential environment that perfectly fits with the character of the place and townscape; an environment complete with most of the facilities necessary for life including medical institutions, child-care facilities and shopping places; a residence-focused development project in which most of the area is allocated for squares and promenades, creating a comfortable and relaxing environment; and a hotel-like condominium fully provided with a range of concierge service as well as a cafe lounge and a relaxation room. In response to demands from residents unsatisfied with simple architectural designs any more, developers have offered many proposals, addressing enhancements and improvements of residential environments incorporating cities as part of them.
Model towns planned in many locations in the cities are leading urban residential life toward the future. They succeed the tradition and culture fostered by the localities and create beautiful cityscapes with a sense of harmony as a new type of residential area thoroughly pursuing amenity.

I would like to thank all the people who again helped me writing and publishing this book. I would like to thank Satoru Ota at Graphic-sha Publishing Co., Ltd who shepherded all of the writing and production efforts, Seiichi Miyasaka for his translation, all the celebrated photographers for their photograph preparations. I appreciate the support of Mr. Yoshiharu Matsumura. And I would like to acknowledge the wonderful design by Ryuichi Tanji.

清水文夫　Fumio Shimizu

1950年島根県生まれ

芝浦工大、A.Aスクール（英国）、ミラノ工科大学（伊国）にて建築を学ぶ。
相田武文設計研究所、マッテオ・トゥン・アーキテクツを経て、1988年（株）清水文夫アーキテクツを設立、現在に至る。

建築、プロダクトデザイン、インテリアデザインの分野で日本、イタリア、ベトナムにて活動している。編著書に「イタリアン・デザイン」、「ブリティッシュ・アーキテクチャー＆インテイア」、「ブリティッシュ・ドローイング」など多数。1989年より「FP」「Kukan」「Japan Avenue」「First Class」「casa nuova」の編集長を歴任。1999年よりUNESCO, UNIDO, JICA, JETROによるベトナム・タイ・ラオスにおける伝統工芸振興のプロジェクト、及びハノイ市の都市計画に参画。現在もタイ・ベトナムにおいて活動を続けている。

Born in Shimane in 1950. Educated at Shibaura Institute of Technology in Tokyo, Architectural Association School of Architecture in London. and Politecnico di Milano. Worked for Takefumi Aida Architects and Associates and Matteo Thun Architetto in Milano.
In1988, Established Shimizu Fumio Architects, working in the separate fields of Architecture, Industrial and Interior design. Published "Italian Design" "British Architecture & Interior" "British drawing" etc. From 1989 editorial director of magazine of "FP" "Kukan" "Japan Avenue" "First Class" "casa nuova".
From 1999, development of traditional crafts in the project of UNESCO, UNIDO, JICA, JETRO and Urban Development in Hanoi in JICA.

DESIGNERS' APARTMENTS in JAPAN
Architect-Designed
High-Rise CONDOMINIUMS

デザイナーズ・マンション Super Selection

発行
　2006年12月25日　初版第1刷発行

編纂
　清水文夫 ©

発行者
　久世利郎

発行所
　株式会社グラフィック社
　〒102-0073
　東京都千代田区九段北1-14-17
　Tel.03-3263-4318／Fax.03-3263-5297
　郵便振替：00130-6-114345
　http://www.graphicsha.co.jp

印刷・製本
　錦明印刷株式会社

© 2006　本書の内容は、著作権上の保護を受けています。著作権者及び出版社の文書による事前の同意を得ずに、本書の内容の一部、あるいは全部を無断で複写複製、転載することは禁じられています。

本書の内容における電話での質問はお受けできませんので、返信葉書同封の上、弊社編集部宛にお送り下さい。

乱丁・落丁はお取り替えいたします。

ISBN4-7661-1713-1 C3052